BEAT
BLACKJACK
NOW!

BEAT BLACKJACK NOW!

The Easiest Way to Get the Edge

Frank Scoblete

TRIUMPH
BOOKS

Library of Congress Cataloging-in-Publication Data

Scoblete, Frank.
  Beat blackjack now! / Frank Scoblete.
      p. cm.
  ISBN-13: 978-1-60078-333-3
  ISBN-10: 1-60078-333-3
  1. Blackjack (Game) I. Title.
  GV1295.B55S357 2010
  795.4'23—dc22

                                        2010014219

This book is available in quantity at special discounts for your group or organization. For further information, contact:

Triumph Books
542 South Dearborn Street
Suite 750
Chicago, Illinois 60605
(312) 939-3330
Fax (312) 663-3557
www.triumphbooks.com

Printed in U.S.A.
ISBN: 978-1-60078-333-3
Design by Patricia Frey

Special thanks:

To Dan Pronovost, who created Speed Count and the Optimum Basic Strategy. His is the glorious burden of genius.

To Henry Tamburin, who brought this great method to me and to the public and taught our seminars in it.

To Dominator, my friend, who has played it with me in the casinos for years.

To Michael Shackleford for his help with Spanish 21 and the simplified Basic Strategy.

To the Speed Count blackjack team that just keeps rolling along using all the advice I give in this book. Keep at it, ladies and gentlemen.

Contents

CHAPTER 1

Yes! *You* Can Beat Blackjack

There are three types of casino blackjack players:

1. The first are the totally, unquestionably stupid, idiotic, hopeless, pathetic, intuitive, dopey players—also labeled as the *ploppies* of the blackjack world—who have no idea that the game can be a close contest between the player and the casino, *if* the players know what they are doing. They even reject the idea that blackjack can be beaten by some advantage players (which you can become by reading this book).

2. The second are the Basic Strategy players, who know the proper strategy for the blackjack games they wish to play and play that strategy perfectly. These players, while not able to get an edge over the casino, keep the casino edge around ½ percent, an expected loss of just 50 cents per $100 wagered. A close contest, not bad at all.

3. The third type are the advantage players; those players who know how to get a real, mathematical edge over the game. These players can beat the game of blackjack and have been beating it for decades now. It used to take some mental strain for most players to learn how to do this, so very few ever got good enough to accomplish achieving an edge. Today? Well today, with this book, any blackjack player can get the edge over the house—a real edge, a mathematically proven edge—and it isn't hard to do.

If you are the Type One player and have no interest in learning the proper Basic Strategy for the game of blackjack, then put this book back on the shelf, because you will need the money you would have spent on it to fuel your considerable losses at the table. Or if you are the type who buys into the deranged strategies of some blackjack gurus who tell you to not split a pair of 8s or aces against every dealer up-card, then you put this book back too.

Truly committed losers do not need a book like this. Why waste your money on learning how to do things right when you can waste much more of it playing wrong? I guess if you like being a ploppy, you must be having a hell of a lot of fun.

If you are already a Type Two player, meaning a strong Basic Strategy blackjack player, then you should consider taking the next step up the blackjack ladder and become an advantage player.

Stop!

Do not say, "Well, I tried card counting in the past, but it was just too hard to learn and much harder to play in the casinos!" That may have been true of the traditional card-counting strategies you tried to learn in days past—such strategies as the Hi-Lo—but you can now say "Hell no!" to such strategies ever since that skinny Canadian genius Dan Pronovost created the easiest method ever developed to get a real edge at the game: Speed Count.

If you already know how to play the game, you can learn Speed Count in 15 minutes, and with a little practice you will be ready to take on the casinos now. *Yes, now!* You won't have to practice for six months as many players do in order to learn the Hi-Lo count and use it effectively in a casino. That same sentence goes for every traditional card-counting system available on the market. Speed Count, coupled with Pronovost's Optimum Basic Strategy (OBS) can give you a real mathematical edge over the casinos—and it is easy to learn and easy to execute in the casinos.

What if you have never played blackjack before? Can this book help you? Absolutely! You can go from a novice to an accomplished player if you follow what is written in these pages. This book will teach you how to play; it will show you the various Basic Strategies for single-deck, double-deck, four-deck, six-deck, and eight-deck games. After you learn and are comfortable playing, you too should consider taking that step into the Speed Count world of advantage play.

There is no reason, other than laziness and/or a joy in losing one's money, that should keep anyone who reads this book from getting a real edge over the house. Why not learn the easiest method to beat the house? Why not become a winner?

There is some little-known and also some never-before-revealed information contained in these pages that will help you cut the house edge even more than what you get by using Basic Strategy. The goal of this book is to really turn the tables on the casinos and ultimately make you their conquerors—without the strain or headaches of traditional systems. With our added and mathematically *proven* material, you can start hacking away at the casino industry just as it hacks away at the hapless, hopeless ploppies who throw their hard-earned money into the casino treasuries when they play blackjack so poorly.

Many important elements set the strategies in this book apart from the strategies you can learn in most other blackjack books. Some of these strategies are unique. I'll repeat: everything in these pages has been proven. There is no wishful thinking here. Just facts and easy-to-learn strategies based on facts. And it is all here, laid out for you.

Beating the casinos doesn't get any easier than this. New players can go from novice to expert, good players can go directly to expert, and expert players can learn things they never imagined before.

Why don't you join the club of advantage players? There's plenty of room for everyone!

CHAPTER 2

How to Play the Game

Blackjack is the most popular casino card game in the world. The player just has to beat the dealer's hand. The player doesn't have to get 21 or even close to 21. Just beat the dealer's hand. To make matters even more fun, there is a big element of skill involved too. It is such skill that allows a good player to keep the casino edge quite low, sometimes under the ½ percent mark, meaning a loss of less than 50 cents per $100 wagered.

Where Blackjack Came From

Even though blackjack has a long history, the origins of the game are not entirely clear. It is widely thought that the precursor to blackjack was *vingt-et-un* (pronounced van-tay-uhn, meaning "twenty and one," or simply "21"), which originated in the French casinos around 1700.

It was so popular that *vingt-et-un* spread throughout the world. The name of the game soon changed depending on where it was being played. In England it became *Van John*, and in Australia it was *Pontoon*. It is generally believed that the game made its way to America in the 1800s, but in America it did not find much popularity in gambling houses. To encourage more players to try it, the casinos changed the rules and began paying a 10-to-1 bonus when a player's initial two cards were either a jack of clubs (a black card) or jack of spades (a black card) together with an ace of spades (a black card), and thus Americans called the game *blackjack*.

Nevada legalized gambling in 1931, and gradually blackjack made its way into legalized casinos in Las Vegas. Over time the rules were changed to pay a 3-to-2 bonus on blackjack, also allowing red jacks and red aces to become blackjacks as well as those higher cards that were black. The casinos also allowed players to *double down* and *pair split*. This increased the popularity of blackjack and fueled the growth of the game.

Objective of the Game

Many players have the misconception that the objective of blackjack is to get as close to 21 as possible without going over. This is not so. The objective is to beat the dealer's hand by:

- Having your hand total higher than the dealer's hand;
- Not going over 21 when the dealer does.
  Going over 21 is called *busting*.

Card Values

- Picture cards count as 10.
- Aces count as one or 11.
- All other cards are valued based on their faces.

Card suits have no meaning in blackjack. The total of any hand is the sum of the card values in the hand. A hand containing a 4-5-8 totals 17. Another containing a queen-5 totals 15. The ace always counts as an 11 initially, but if a player draws one (or more) cards and the hand totals over 21, then the ace can be counted as 1. For example, 4-ace-8 counts as 13, because counting the ace as 11 would bust the player.

Soft Hands and Hard Hands

Any hand that counts the ace as 11 is known as a *soft hand*; ace-7 is a soft 18 and ace-3-3 is a Soft 17. A *hard hand* is any hand that either does *not* contain an ace, or if it does, the ace counts as 1; 10-8 and 5-ace-10-2 are hard 18 hands. Soft hands are played differently than hard hands.

Number of Players

Blackjack tables can accommodate from one up to five, six, or seven players, and it doesn't make any difference which seat you take, because

Blackjack layout.

players are competing against the casino dealer's hand and not against each other's hands. The cards are always dealt by the casino dealer.

Playing With Chips

Casinos prefer that players bet with casino chips, also known as *cheques*, rather than with cash, although some venues allow cash play and some do not. Dealers will call out, "Money plays!" for a player betting cash. To convert your cash to casino chips, wait until the dealer completes the hand in progress, and then place your cash on the layout *in front* of your betting spot. The dealer will exchange your cash for an equivalent amount of casino chips, which you then place in front of you.

> **Please Note:** *Some casinos don't allow players to enter midgame. If this is the case, wait until the dealer finishes the deck(s), or shoe, and begins to reshuffle before you place your cash on the table for chips or your chips in the betting circle in front of you. This rule is called "no mid-shoe entry."*

Chip Denomination

Chips have denominations printed on them, and they are also color-coded. The most common casino-chip colors/denominations are:

- Blue or White = $1
- Pink = $2.50
- Red = $5
- Green = $25
- Black = $100
- Purple = $500
- Burgundy or Orange = $1,000
- Silver or Gold = $2,000
- Brown = $5,000

Betting Limits

Before you sit down at a blackjack table, know what the table's betting limits are. There is a small display on the table, usually to the dealer's right (your left), that will tell you the table minimum and maximum bets, and it will usually tell you the rules of the game.

A table with a $10 *minimum* betting requirement means that you must wager at least $10 on each hand. If a table has a $1,000 *maximum*, this means you are not allowed to make your initial wager more than $1,000. You are permitted in most casinos to wager more than one spot, but some casinos might require you to bet at least twice the table minimum on each spot.

Casino rules are not carved in stone. Some casinos will allow you to bet the same table minimum on two hands—if you ask the pit boss (nicely). "Just ask" is a good policy to see if you can get the casino to offer you a better game. This is often called *pushing the house*.

> **Please Note:** *Basic Strategy players should not risk money on two spots, as this only doubles, sometimes quadruples, their expected losses.*

Number of Decks

From one to eight decks are used to play blackjack. Single-deck and double-deck games are usually dealt by hand, although on some

Blackjack shoe. *Photo courtesy of Getty Images*

occasions such games might be dealt face-up or from a *shoe*, which is a box to hold the cards. On four-deck, six-deck, and eight-deck games casinos almost always use a shoe.

The Deal

Prior to the deal of the cards, all players must make a bet by placing chips in their respective betting spots. Every player and the dealer will receive two cards. One of the dealer's cards, known as the *up-card*, is dealt face up so that players can see its value. The other dealer's card, known as the dealer's *down-card* or *hole card*, is unseen.

The two player cards can be dealt either face up, face down, or sometimes one up and one down. In general, in games that are dealt from shoes, the players' cards are dealt face up. In this case you should not touch the cards. In games in which the dealer deals from his hand by pitching the cards to the players, the players' cards are usually dealt face down. However, in some casinos that use double deck, both cards are dealt face up. When the cards are dealt face down, it is permissible for the player to handle the cards with *one hand* only, and the cards must always be held above the table.

Blackjacks

When a player is dealt an ace and a 10-valued card as his first two cards, it is called a *blackjack* or *natural* and generally is paid one and one-half times the original bet, meaning a 3-to-2 payoff.

> **Please Note:** *Some casinos pay 6-to-5 on player blackjacks, which gives the casino a much higher edge over players. A normal blackjack game will pay $15 for $10 on a blackjack; an "abnormal" game will pay $12 to $10 for a blackjack. These games should be avoided. In blackjack we all want to be normal.*

Push

When your hand totals the same as the dealer, this is known as a *push*, or tie, and you get to keep your bet.

Player's Action

If the dealer doesn't have a blackjack, players have to make a decision on how they want to play their hands. Players' options include the following:

Hit: This means you want the dealer to give you another card. In a game where the initial two player cards are dealt face up, if you want a hit, make a beckoning motion with your finger, or tap the table behind your cards with your finger. In a game where the cards are dealt face down (i.e., usually a single- or double-deck game), you signify to the dealer that you want a hit by scratching the edges of the cards lightly on the felt.

Hitting hand signal in a face-up game.

Scratching for a hit in a face-down game.

Stand: This means you are satisfied with the total of the hand and want to stand with the cards you have. In face-up games, indicate that you want to stand by waving your hand over the cards. In face-down games, tuck your cards under the chips that you wagered in your betting spot.

Standing hand signal in a face-up game.

Putting cards under chips to stand in a face-down game.

Doubling Down: This playing option allows you to double your bet on your first two cards and receive one additional card. In most casinos you can double down only after you receive your first two cards and before drawing another card. To signal to the dealer that you want to double down, just place your chip(s) next to the original chip(s) bet on the hand. In face-down games, you must toss your cards on the table face up and then make the secondary double-down wager.

Doubling down.

In face-up games, simply make the secondary double-down bet as previously. Most casinos allow players to *double for less*, which means you can wager less than the original bet when you make the secondary double-down bet. In a face-up game, the draw card on a double-down is usually placed perpendicular to the initial two cards. In a face-down game, the dealer will place the draw card either face down or face up.

Pair-Splitting: If you are dealt two cards of the same rank (say, a pair of 6s or aces), you could exercise the option to split. When you split, you must make another bet equal to your original bet by placing your chip(s) next to the original bet. By pair-splitting you play each card as a separate hand, and you can draw as many cards as you like to each hand with the exception of split aces. Most casinos will allow only one draw card to each ace because it is such a powerful card.

Splitting a pair.

Here is an example of splitting: If you are dealt a pair of 8s (16) and split, you would have two separate hands containing an 8. You would be required to play out one of the split hands first before taking any action on the other hand. In face-down games you indicate that you want to split by placing another chip next to the initial chip and turn over your cards. In face-up games, toss your chips on the table and then make the secondary wager. Most casinos will allow players to split all 10-value cards such as a jack-10 or queen-king, although this is not a recommended playing strategy. Also some casinos will allow a player to resplit up to a total of four hands. Most casinos also allow players to double down after pair-splitting, which is a player-favorable rule. Keep in mind that if you split aces and receive a 10 to an ace, you have a 21 and *not* a blackjack.

Surrender: A rare option. Surrender allows a player to forfeit his initial hand with an automatic loss of half the original bet. Players can surrender their initial two-card hands only after the dealer has checked to see if she herself has a blackjack. After a player draws a third card, the surrender option is no longer available. If the dealer has a blackjack hand, then surrender is not available. A player can signify to the dealer that he wants to surrender by simply saying to the dealer, "surrender." Some casinos have implemented a hand signal for surrender, which is to use your finger and draw an imaginary line from left to right across the felt layout. When a player surrenders, the dealer will remove the player's cards from the table and place one-half of the player's bet in the chip rack. The player is no longer involved in that round.

Early Surrender: The abominable snowman of blackjack options—rarely if ever seen in American casinos. It is highly player-friendly. With early surrender, a player can surrender his hand *before* the dealer checks to see if she has blackjack, and the player does not lose his entire bet if she has one. The playing strategy for early surrender is much different than late surrender.

Insurance: When the dealer's up-card is an ace, the dealer will ask players if they want to make the insurance wager. Insurance is a side bet where players are betting that the dealer's hole card will be a 10-valued card. Players can make an insurance bet equal to one-half of their initial bet made on the hand. To make the insurance bet, you simply place your chips on the insurance line, which is located right above the player betting spot. You win your insurance bet if the dealer has a 10-value card in the hole. A winning insurance bet pays off at 2-to-1 odds.

Even Money: When the player has a blackjack hand and the dealer has an ace showing, the dealer will ask the player if he wants "even money." Even money means the dealer will automatically give you a 1-to-1 (or even money) payoff on your bet before he checks his down-card for a potential blackjack. Taking even money yields the same result as making an insurance bet on your blackjack hand.

No-Hole Card: In many casinos outside the U.S., the dealer does not take her second card until after all players have completed acting on their hands. The no-hole-card rule has no effect on the odds of the game or on the basic playing strategy. However, in some European casinos, players will lose both of their wagers made on splitting and doubling when the dealer's second card gives her a blackjack. The latter is known as the European No-Hole-Card Rule (abbreviated ENHC), and this does require a slight change in playing strategy.

Busting: If a player's hand exceeds 21, he has busted and loses the hand regardless of the dealer's total. When a player busts, his cards and his bet are immediately collected by the dealer. This factor is why the casino has the mathematical edge over players. If a player busts, he loses even if the dealer subsequently busts in the same round.

Dealer's Playing Strategy: Unlike players, the dealer in blackjack has no playing options. Casino rules specify that a dealer must draw when the dealer's hand totals less than 17 and stand when the total is 17 to 21. In some casinos, dealers must stand on Soft 17 (ace-6), and in other casinos they must hit Soft 17. Not hitting Soft 17 is better for the player.

Shuffle Machines: Many casinos use automatic shufflers to shuffle the cards in multiple-deck games. Usually the dealer will use, say, six decks of cards while a different set of six decks of cards is being shuffled by an automatic shuffling device. When the cut-card appears in the shoe being dealt, the dealer will complete that round and then switch the two sets of cards so the newly shuffled cards are put into play while the completed set of cards is placed in the automatic shuffler.

Automatic shufflers eliminate the downtime that occurs when the dealer manually shuffles the cards. Another type of automatic shuffler is known as a *continuous shuffling machine* (CSM). With this device the discards from one round are placed back into the shuffler to be mixed with the undealt decks of cards. With a CSM there is never a pause in action, and more hands are dealt per hour than with an automatic shuffler, resulting in a slightly higher theoretical hourly loss rate for average players.

Please Note: *The more hands you play, the more the house edge will eat away at your bankroll. It is better to play where the dealers shuffle by hand; next best is where dealers use an automatic shuffler; but never, NEVER play where they use a continuous shuffle machine. Continuous shufflers will increase by about 20 percent the number of hands a player receives in an hour.*

CHAPTER 3

Basic Strategies for Blackjack

Even if you do not wish to become an advantage player, using the following Basic Strategies make blackjack a very close contest. You can memorize the strategies or, to make it really easy, you can photocopy each on a piece of paper, shrink-wrap it, and you are ready to go. Almost all casinos will allow players to refer to Basic Strategy charts. Or you can buy smaller, plastic cards from www.smartgaming.com. (DO NOT use the Optimum Basic Strategies that are used for Speed Count.)

S=Stand; H=Hit; D=Double Down; P=Split; U=Surrender
Game is 4-6-8 decks; dealer STANDS on 17; double after splits allowed

For boxes with a a slash, use play on the left if permitted; if not, use play on the right.

Hand	2	3	4	5	6	7	8	9	10	Ace
8	H	H	H	H	H	H	H	H	H	H
9	H	D/H	D/H	D/H	D/H	H	H	H	H	H
10	D/H	D/H	D/H	D/H	D/H	D/H	D/H	D/H	H	H
11	D/H	D/H	D/H	D/H	D/H	D/H	D/H	D/H	D/H	H
12	H	H	S	S	S	H	H	H	H	H
13	S	S	S	S	S	H	H	H	H	H
14	S	S	S	S	S	H	H	H	H	H

Hand	2	3	4	5	6	7	8	9	10	Ace
15	S	S	S	S	S	H	H	H	U/H	H
16	S	S	S	S	S	H	H	U/H	U/H	U/H
17	S	S	S	S	S	S	S	S	S	S
A-2	H	H	H	D/H	D/H	H	H	H	H	H
A-3	H	H	H	D/H	D/H	H	H	H	H	H
A-4	H	H	D/H	D/H	D/H	H	H	H	H	H
A-5	H	H	D/H	D/H	D/H	H	H	H	H	H
A-6	H	D/H	D/H	D/H	D/H	H	H	H	H	H
A-7	H	D/S	D/S	D/S	D/S	S	S	H	H	H
A-8	S	S	S	S	S	S	S	S	S	S
A-9	S	S	S	S	S	S	S	S	S	S
A-A	P	P	P	P	P	P	P	P	P	P
2-2	P	P	P	P	P	P	H	H	H	H
3-3	P	P	P	P	P	P	H	H	H	H
4-4	H	H	H	P	P	H	H	H	H	H
5-5	D/H	D/H	D/H	D/H	D/H	D/H	D/H	D/H	H	H
6-6	P	P	P	P	P	H	H	H	H	H
7-7	P	P	P	P	P	P	H	H	H	H
8-8	P	P	P	P	P	P	P	P	P	P
9-9	P	P	P	P	P	S	P	P	S	S
10-10	S	S	S	S	S	S	S	S	S	S

S=Stand; H=Hit; D=Double Down; P=Split; U=Surrender

Game is 4-6-8 decks; dealer STANDS on 17; no double after splits allowed

For boxes with a slash, use play on the left if permitted; if not, use play on the right.

Hand	2	3	4	5	6	7	8	9	10	Ace
8	H	H	H	H	H	H	H	H	H	H
9	H	D/H	D/H	D/H	D/H	H	H	H	H	H
10	D/H	D/H	D/H	D/H	D/H	D/H	D/H	D/H	H	H
11	D/H	D/H	D/H	D/H	D/H	D/H	D/H	D/H	D/H	H
12	H	H	S	S	S	H	H	H	H	H
13	S	S	S	S	S	H	H	H	H	H
14	S	S	S	S	S	H	H	H	H	H
15	S	S	S	S	S	H	H	H	U/H	H
16	S	S	S	S	S	H	H	U/H	U/H	U/H
17	S	S	S	S	S	S	S	S	S	S
A-2	H	H	H	D/H	D/H	H	H	H	H	H
A-3	H	H	H	D/H	D/H	H	H	H	H	H
A-4	H	H	D/H	D/H	D/H	H	H	H	H	H
A-5	H	H	D/H	D/H	D/H	H	H	H	H	H
A-6	H	D/H	D/H	D/H	D/H	H	H	H	H	H
A-7	S	D/S	D/S	D/S	D/S	S	S	H	H	H
A-8	S	S	S	S	S	S	S	S	S	S
A-9	S	S	S	S	S	S	S	S	S	S
A-A	P	P	P	P	P	P	P	P	P	P
2-2	H	H	P	P	P	P	H	H	H	H
3-3	H	H	P	P	P	P	H	H	H	H
4-4	H	H	H	P	P	H	H	H	H	H
5-5	D/H	D/H	D/H	D/H	D/H	D/H	D/H	D/H	H	H
6-6	H	P	P	P	P	H	H	H	H	H
7-7	P	P	P	P	P	P	H	H	H	H
8-8	P	P	P	P	P	P	P	P	P	P
9-9	P	P	P	P	P	S	P	P	S	S
10-10	S	S	S	S	S	S	S	S	S	S

S=Stand; H=Hit; D=Double Down; P=Split; U=Surrender
Game is 4-6-8 decks; dealer HITS on Soft 17 (Ace-6); double after splits allowed

For boxes with a slash, use play on the left if permitted; if not, use play on the right.

Hand	2	3	4	5	6	7	8	9	10	Ace
8	H	H	H	H	H	H	H	H	H	H
9	H	D/H	D/H	D/H	D/H	H	H	H	H	H
10	D/H	D/H	D/H	D/H	D/H	D/H	D/H	D/H	H	H
11	D/H	D/H	D/H	D/H	D/H	D/H	D/H	D/H	D/H	D/H
12	H	H	S	S	S	H	H	H	H	H
13	S	S	S	S	S	H	H	H	H	H
14	S	S	S	S	S	H	H	H	H	H
15	S	S	S	S	S	H	H	H	U/H	H
16	S	S	S	S	S	H	H	U/H	U/H	U/H
17	S	S	S	S	S	S	S	S	S	U/S
A-2	H	H	H	D/H	D/H	H	H	H	H	H
A-3	H	H	H	D/H	D/H	H	H	H	H	H
A-4	H	H	D/H	D/H	D/H	H	H	H	H	H
A-5	H	H	D/H	D/H	D/H	H	H	H	H	H
A-6	H	D/H	D/H	D/H	D/H	H	H	H	H	H
A-7	D/S	D/S	D/S	D/S	D/S	S	S	H	H	H
A-8	S	S	S	S	D/S	S	S	S	S	S
A-9	S	S	S	S	S	S	S	S	S	S
A-A	P	P	P	P	P	P	P	P	P	P
2-2	P	P	P	P	P	P	H	H	H	H
3-3	P	P	P	P	P	P	H	H	H	H
4-4	H	H	H	P	P	H	H	H	H	H
5-5	D/H	D/H	D/H	D/H	D/H	D/H	D/H	D/H	H	H
6-6	P	P	P	P	P	H	H	H	H	H
7-7	P	P	P	P	P	P	H	H	H	H
8-8	P	P	P	P	P	P	P	P	P	P
9-9	P	P	P	P	P	S	P	P	S	S
10-10	S	S	S	S	S	S	S	S	S	S

S=Stand; H=Hit; D=Double Down; P=Split; U=Surrender

Game is 4-6-8 decks; dealer HITS on Soft 17 (Ace-6); no double after splits allowed

For boxes with a slash, use play on the left if permitted; if not, use play on the right.

Hand	2	3	4	5	6	7	8	9	10	Ace
8	H	H	H	H	H	H	H	H	H	H
9	H	D/H	D/H	D/H	D/H	H	H	H	H	H
10	D/H	D/H	D/H	D/H	D/H	D/H	D/H	D/H	H	H
11	D/H	D/H	D/H	D/H	D/H	D/H	D/H	D/H	D/H	D/H
12	H	H	S	S	S	H	H	H	H	H
13	S	S	S	S	S	H	H	H	H	H
14	S	S	S	S	S	H	H	H	H	H
15	S	S	S	S	S	H	H	H	U/H	H
16	S	S	S	S	S	H	H	U/H	U/H	U/H
17	S	S	S	S	S	S	S	S	S	U/S
A-2	H	H	H	D/H	D/H	H	H	H	H	H
A-3	H	H	H	D/H	D/H	H	H	H	H	H
A-4	H	H	D/H	D/H	D/H	H	H	H	H	H
A-5	H	H	D/H	D/H	D/H	H	H	H	H	H
A-6	H	D/H	D/H	D/H	D/H	H	H	H	H	H
A-7	D/S	D/S	D/S	D/S	D/S	S	S	H	H	H
A-8	S	S	S	S	D/S	S	S	S	S	S
A-9	S	S	S	S	S	S	S	S	S	S
A-A	P	P	P	P	P	P	P	P	P	P
2-2	H	H	P	P	P	P	H	H	H	H
3-3	H	H	P	P	P	P	H	H	H	H
4-4	H	H	H	H	H	H	H	H	H	H
5-5	D/H	D/H	D/H	D/H	D/H	D/H	D/H	D/H	H	H
6-6	H	P	P	P	P	H	H	H	H	H
7-7	P	P	P	P	P	P	H	H	H	H
8-8	P	P	P	P	P	P	P	P	P	P
9-9	P	P	P	P	P	S	P	P	S	S
10-10	S	S	S	S	S	S	S	S	S	S

S=Stand; H=Hit; D=Double Down; P=Split; U=Surrender
Game is DOUBLE decks; dealer STANDS on 17; double after splits allowed
   For boxes with a slash, use play on the left if permitted; if not, use play on the right.

Hand	2	3	4	5	6	7	8	9	10	Ace
8	H	H	H	H	H	H	H	H	H	H
9	D/H	D/H	D/H	D/H	D/H	H	H	H	H	H
10	D/H	D/H	D/H	D/H	D/H	D/H	D/H	D/H	H	H
11	D/H	D/H	D/H	D/H	D/H	D/H	D/H	D/H	D/H	D/H
12	H	H	S	S	S	H	H	H	H	H
13	S	S	S	S	S	H	H	H	H	H
14	S	S	S	S	S	H	H	H	H	H
15	S	S	S	S	S	H	H	H	U/H	H
16	S	S	S	S	S	H	H	H	U/H	U/H
17	S	S	S	S	S	S	S	S	S	S
A-2	H	H	H	D/H	D/H	H	H	H	H	H
A-3	H	H	H	D/H	D/H	H	H	H	H	H
A-4	H	H	D/H	D/H	D/H	H	H	H	H	H
A-5	H	H	D/H	D/H	D/H	H	H	H	H	H
A-6	H	D/H	D/H	D/H	D/H	H	H	H	H	H
A-7	H	D/S	D/S	D/S	D/S	S	S	H	H	H
A-8	S	S	S	S	S	S	S	S	S	S
A-9	S	S	S	S	S	S	S	S	S	S
A-A	P	P	P	P	P	P	P	P	P	P
2-2	P	P	P	P	P	P	H	H	H	H
3-3	P	P	P	P	P	P	H	H	H	H
4-4	H	H	H	P	P	H	H	H	H	H
5-5	D/H	D/H	D/H	D/H	D/H	D/H	D/H	D/H	H	H
6-6	P	P	P	P	P	P	H	H	H	H
7-7	P	P	P	P	P	P	P/H	H	H	H
8-8	P	P	P	P	P	P	P	P	P	P
9-9	P	P	P	P	P	S	P	P	S	S
10-10	S	S	S	S	S	S	S	S	S	S

S=Stand; H=Hit; D=Double Down; P=Split; U=Surrender

Game is DOUBLE decks; dealer STANDS on 17; no double after splits allowed

For boxes with a slash, use play on the left if permitted; if not, use play on the right.

Hand	2	3	4	5	6	7	8	9	10	Ace
8	H	H	H	H	H	H	H	H	H	H
9	D/H	D/H	D/H	D/H	D/H	H	H	H	H	H
10	D/H	D/H	D/H	D/H	D/H	D/H	D/H	D/H	H	H
11	D/H	D/H	D/H	D/H	D/H	D/H	D/H	D/H	D/H	D/H
12	H	H	S	S	S	H	H	H	H	H
13	S	S	S	S	S	H	H	H	H	H
14	S	S	S	S	S	H	H	H	H	H
15	S	S	S	S	S	H	H	H	U/H	H
16	S	S	S	S	S	H	H	H	U/H	U/H
17	S	S	S	S	S	S	S	S	S	S
A-2	H	H	H	D/H	D/H	H	H	H	H	H
A-3	H	H	H	D/H	D/H	H	H	H	H	H
A-4	H	H	D/H	D/H	D/H	H	H	H	H	H
A-5	H	H	D/H	D/H	D/H	H	H	H	H	H
A-6	H	D/H	D/H	D/H	D/H	H	H	H	H	H
A-7	S	D/S	D/S	D/S	D/S	S	S	H	H	H
A-8	S	S	S	S	S	S	S	S	S	S
A-9	S	S	S	S	S	S	S	S	S	S
A-A	P	P	P	P	P	P	P	P	P	P
2-2	H	H	P	P	P	P	H	H	H	H
3-3	H	H	P	P	P	P	H	H	H	H
4-4	H	H	H	H	H	H	H	H	H	H
5-5	D/H	D/H	D/H	D/H	D/H	D/H	D/H	D/H	H	H
6-6	P	P	P	P	P	H	H	H	H	H
7-7	P	P	P	P	P	P	H	H	H	H
8-8	P	P	P	P	P	P	P	P	P	P
9-9	P	P	P	P	P	S	P	P	S	S
10-10	S	S	S	S	S	S	S	S	S	S

S=Stand; H=Hit; D=Double Down; P=Split; U=Surrender

Game is DOUBLE decks; dealer HITS on Soft 17 (Ace-6); double after splits allowed

For boxes with a slash, use play on the left if permitted; if not, use play on the right.

Hand	2	3	4	5	6	7	8	9	10	Ace
8	H	H	H	H	H	H	H	H	H	H
9	D/H	D/H	D/H	D/H	D/H	H	H	H	H	H
10	D/H	D/H	D/H	D/H	D/H	D/H	D/H	D/H	H	H
11	D/H	D/H	D/H	D/H	D/H	D/H	D/H	D/H	D/H	D/H
12	H	H	S	S	S	H	H	H	H	H
13	S	S	S	S	S	H	H	H	H	H
14	S	S	S	S	S	H	H	H	H	H
15	S	S	S	S	S	H	H	H	U/H	U/H
16	S	S	S	S	S	H	H	H	U/H	U/H
17	S	S	S	S	S	S	S	S	S	U/S
A-2	H	H	H	D/H	D/H	H	H	H	H	H
A-3	H	H	D/H	D/H	D/H	H	H	H	H	H
A-4	H	H	D/H	D/H	D/H	H	H	H	H	H
A-5	H	H	D/H	D/H	D/H	H	H	H	H	H
A-6	H	D/H	D/H	D/H	D/H	H	H	H	H	H
A-7	D/S	D/S	D/S	D/S	D/S	S	S	H	H	H
A-8	S	S	S	S	D/S	S	S	S	S	S
A-9	S	S	S	S	S	S	S	S	S	S
A-A	P	P	P	P	P	P	P	P	P	P
2-2	P	P	P	P	P	P	H	H	H	H
3-3	P	P	P	P	P	P	H	H	H	H
4-4	H	H	H	P	P	H	H	H	H	H
5-5	D/H	D/H	D/H	D/H	D/H	D/H	D/H	D/H	H	H
6-6	P	P	P	P	P	P	H	H	H	H
7-7	P	P	P	P	P	P	P	H	H	H
8-8	P	P	P	P	P	P	P	P	P	P
9-9	P	P	P	P	P	S	P	P	S	S
10-10	S	S	S	S	S	S	S	S	S	S

S=Stand; H=Hit; D=Double Down; P=Split; U=Surrender
Game is DOUBLE decks; dealer HITS on Soft 17 (Ace-6); no double after splits allowed

For boxes with a slash, use play on the left if permitted; if not, use play on the right.

Hand	2	3	4	5	6	7	8	9	10	Ace
8	H	H	H	H	H	H	H	H	H	H
9	D/H	D/H	D/H	D/H	D/H	H	H	H	H	H
10	D/H	D/H	D/H	D/H	D/H	D/H	D/H	D/H	H	H
11	D/H	D/H	D/H	D/H	D/H	D/H	D/H	D/H	D/H	D/H
12	H	H	S	S	S	H	H	H	H	H
13	S	S	S	S	S	H	H	H	H	H
14	S	S	S	S	S	H	H	H	H	H
15	S	S	S	S	S	H	H	H	U/H	U/H
16	S	S	S	S	S	H	H	H	U/H	U/H
17	S	S	S	S	S	S	S	S	S	U/S
A-2	H	H	H	D/H	D/H	H	H	H	H	H
A-3	H	H	D/H	D/H	D/H	H	H	H	H	H
A-4	H	H	D/H	D/H	D/H	H	H	H	H	H
A-5	H	H	D/H	D/H	D/H	H	H	H	H	H
A-6	H	D/H	D/H	D/H	D/H	H	H	H	H	H
A-7	D/S	D/S	D/S	D/S	D/S	S	S	H	H	H
A-8	S	S	S	S	D/S	S	S	S	S	S
A-9	S	S	S	S	S	S	S	S	S	S
A-A	P	P	P	P	P	P	P	P	P	P
2-2	H	H	P	P	P	P	H	H	H	H
3-3	H	H	P	P	P	P	H	H	H	H
4-4	H	H	H	H	H	H	H	H	H	H
5-5	D/H	D/H	D/H	D/H	D/H	D/H	D/H	D/H	H	H
6-6	P	P	P	P	P	H	H	H	H	H
7-7	P	P	P	P	P	P	H	H	H	H
8-8	P	P	P	P	P	P	P	P	P	P
9-9	P	P	P	P	P	S	P	P	S	S
10-10	S	S	S	S	S	S	S	S	S	S

S=Stand; H=Hit; D=Double Down; P=Split; U=Surrender

Game is SINGLE deck; dealer STANDS on 17; double after splits allowed

For boxes with a slash, use play on the left if permitted; if not, use play on the right.

Hand	2	3	4	5	6	7	8	9	10	Ace
8	H	H	H	D/H	D/H	H	H	H	H	H
9	D/H	D/H	D/H	D/H	D/H	H	H	H	H	H
10	D/H	D/H	D/H	D/H	D/H	D/H	D/H	D/H	H	H
11	D/H	D/H	D/H	D/H	D/H	D/H	D/H	D/H	D/H	D/H
12	H	H	S	S	S	H	H	H	H	H
13	S	S	S	S	S	H	H	H	H	H
14	S	S	S	S	S	H	H	H	H	H
15	S	S	S	S	S	H	H	H	H	H
16	S	S	S	S	S	H	H	H	U/H	U/H
17	S	S	S	S	S	S	S	S	S	S
A-2	H	H	D/H	D/H	D/H	H	H	H	H	H
A-3	H	H	D/H	D/H	D/H	H	H	H	H	H
A-4	H	H	D/H	D/H	D/H	H	H	H	H	H
A-5	H	H	D/H	D/H	D/H	H	H	H	H	H
A-6	D/H	D/H	D/H	D/H	D/H	H	H	H	H	H
A-7	S	D/S	D/S	D/S	D/S	S	S	H	H	S
A-8	S	S	S	S	D/S	S	S	S	S	S
A-9	S	S	S	S	S	S	S	S	S	S
A-A	P	P	P	P	P	P	P	P	P	P
2-2	P	P	P	P	P	P	H	H	H	H
3-3	P	P	P	P	P	P	P	H	H	H
4-4	H	H	P	P	P	H	H	H	H	H
5-5	D/H	D/H	D/H	D/H	D/H	D/H	D/H	D/H	H	H
6-6	P	P	P	P	P	P	H	H	H	H
7-7	P	P	P	P	P	P	P	H	U/S	H
8-8	P	P	P	P	P	P	P	P	P	P
9-9	P	P	P	P	P	S	P	P	S	S
10-10	S	S	S	S	S	S	S	S	S	S

S=Stand; H=Hit; D=Double Down; P=Split; U=Surrender

Game is SINGLE deck; dealer HITS on Soft 17 (Ace-6); no double after splits allowed

For boxes with a slash, use play on the left if permitted; if not, use play on the right.

Hand	2	3	4	5	6	7	8	9	10	Ace
8	H	H	H	D/H	D/H	H	H	H	H	H
9	D/H	D/H	D/H	D/H	D/H	H	H	H	H	H
10	D/H	D/H	D/H	D/H	D/H	D/H	D/H	D/H	H	H
11	D/H	D/H	D/H	D/H	D/H	D/H	D/H	D/H	D/H	D/H
12	H	H	S	S	S	H	H	H	H	H
13	S	S	S	S	S	H	H	H	H	H
14	S	S	S	S	S	H	H	H	H	H
15	S	S	S	S	S	H	H	H	U/H	H
16	S	S	S	S	S	H	H	H	U/H	U/H
17	S	S	S	S	S	S	S	S	S	U/S
A-2	H	H	D/H	D/H	D/H	H	H	H	H	H
A-3	H	H	D/H	D/H	D/H	H	H	H	H	H
A-4	H	H	D/H	D/H	D/H	H	H	H	H	H
A-5	H	H	D/H	D/H	D/H	H	H	H	H	H
A-6	D/H	D/H	D/H	D/H	D/H	H	H	H	H	H
A-7	S	D/S	D/S	D/S	D/S	S	S	H	H	S
A-8	S	S	S	S	D/S	S	S	S	S	S
A-9	S	S	S	S	S	S	S	S	S	S
A-A	P	P	P	P	P	P	P	P	P	P
2-2	H	P	P	P	P	P	H	H	H	H
3-3	H	H	P	P	P	P	H	H	H	H
4-4	H	H	H	D/H	D/H	H	H	H	H	H
5-5	D/H	D/H	D/H	D/H	D/H	D/H	D/H	D/H	H	H
6-6	P	P	P	P	P	H	H	H	H	H
7-7	P	P	P	P	P	P	H	H	U/S	U/H
8-8	P	P	P	P	P	P	P	P	P	P
9-9	P	P	P	P	P	S	P	P	S	S
10-10	S	S	S	S	S	S	S	S	S	S

S=Stand; H=Hit; D=Double Down; P=Split; U=Surrender
Game is SINGLE deck; dealer STANDS on 17; no double after splits allowed

For boxes with a slash, use play on the left if permitted; if not, use play on the right.

Hand	2	3	4	5	6	7	8	9	10	Ace
8	H	H	H	D/H	D/H	H	H	H	H	H
9	D/H	D/H	D/H	D/H	D/H	H	H	H	H	H
10	D/H	D/H	D/H	D/H	D/H	D/H	D/H	D/H	H	H
11	D/H	D/H	D/H	D/H	D/H	D/H	D/H	D/H	D/H	D/H
12	H	H	S	S	S	H	H	H	H	H
13	S	S	S	S	S	H	H	H	H	H
14	S	S	S	S	S	H	H	H	H	H
15	S	S	S	S	S	H	H	H	H	H
16	S	S	S	S	S	H	H	H	U/H	U/S
17	S	S	S	S	S	S	S	S	S	S
A-2	H	H	D/H	D/H	D/H	H	H	H	H	H
A-3	H	H	D/H	D/H	D/H	H	H	H	H	H
A-4	H	H	D/H	D/H	D/H	H	H	H	H	H
A-5	H	H	D/H	D/H	D/H	H	H	H	H	H
A-6	D/H	D/H	D/H	D/H	D/H	H	H	H	H	H
A-7	S	D/S	D/S	D/S	D/S	S	S	H	H	S
A-8	S	S	S	S	D/S	S	S	S	S	S
A-9	S	S	S	S	S	S	S	S	S	S
A-A	P	P	P	P	P	P	P	P	P	P
2-2	H	P	P	P	P	P	H	H	H	H
3-3	H	H	P	P	P	P	H	H	H	H
4-4	H	H	H	D/H	D/H	H	H	H	H	H
5-5	D/H	D/H	D/H	D/H	D/H	D/H	D/H	D/H	H	H
6-6	P	P	P	P	P	H	H	H	H	H
7-7	P	P	P	P	P	P	H	H	U/S	H
8-8	P	P	P	P	P	P	P	P	P	P
9-9	P	P	P	P	P	S	P	P	S	S
10-10	S	S	S	S	S	S	S	S	S	S

CHAPTER 4

Advanced Strategies for Basic Strategy Players

Author's Note: Henry Tamburin did the bulk of the research on this chapter, relying heavily on Fred Renzey's groundbreaking work.

It's no secret that the basic playing strategy is the optimal way to play your hand when the only information you consider is your hand total and the dealer's up-card. This scientifically accurate strategy will cut the house edge to a measly ½ percent or so, depending upon the precise rules. But, you can do even better than this by employing some *advanced* Basic Strategy plays.

Suppose you are a dealt a 16 against a dealer's 10, a very common hand, and surrender is not available? The traditional basic playing strategy says to hit your 16, because in the long run you will lose less money compared to standing. However, what the traditional Basic Strategy doesn't consider is the *makeup* of the hand. It turns out that there is a difference between a hand that totals 16 consisting of a two-card 10-6 or 9-7 and another containing, for example, a three-card 4-5-7. Yes, both hands total 16, but with the three-card 16, you are better off standing, whereas with the two-card 16, you should hit.

The reason you should stand on a 16 when your hand contains three or more cards is because your hand contains one (or more) small-value cards that are no longer available in the pack of un-played cards. These small cards are exactly what you need to make a pat hand when you hit your 16. The fact that a few of them are not available because they are already in your hand is just enough to shift the odds toward standing rather than hitting.

Based on computer studies, it makes sense to stand on all multi-card 16s against a dealer's 10 up-card.

Another hand where your strategy is dependent upon the makeup of the cards is a starting total of 12 against a dealer's 4 up-card. Traditional Basic Strategy states to stand on 12 against a dealer 4. However, there are, in fact, four different ways to be dealt a 12: 10-2, 9-3, 8-4, and 7-5 (6-6 would be considered a pair to be split), and in the specific case of 10-2, you are slightly better off hitting against the dealer's 4, whereas with 9-3, 8-4, and 7-5, you are better off standing.

Another advanced playing technique that can further reduce the house edge is to make a bet on another player's hand. You might think this is a strange play, but it is perfectly legal as long as the player allows you to make such a bet. Why would you want to bet on another player's hand? Because with some hands, a player might have a big edge and not realize it, allowing you the opportunity to take advantage of the situation.

Fred Renzey calls this technique "hand interaction," and he describes several of them in his book, *Blackjack Blue Book*. Here's an example.

Suppose the player next to you bets $20 and is dealt a 7-4 against a dealer's 10. The player might know that the Basic Strategy for this play is to double down, but he may be reluctant to push out another $20 with the dealer showing a 10, so instead he shoves out $10 worth of chips and doubles for less. According to Renzey, "This is when you should spring into action, toss $10 in chips to him, and tell him, I'll go with you on this one, partner."

Essentially, your $10 is riding on the outcome of your fellow player's hand. But, according to Renzey, "You are a 9 percent favorite, so if the player doesn't know enough to take the whole advantage to himself, go ahead and take the rest." Renzey adds, "Getting in one extra double down per half hour for the same amount as your own bets will reduce the house edge by about 0.15 percent."

Here's another hand interaction described by Renzey involving pair splitting. Suppose a fellow player splits a pair of 7s against a dealer 6 and draws another 7. The player should resplit, but suppose he hesitates to put out more money. According to Renzey, "Since a 7 against a dealer 6 is an outright moneymaker, you should quickly toss a bet to him and offer to absorb the cost of splitting that third 7. You are a 3 percent favorite, and if doubling after pair splitting is allowed, you'll have a solid 10 percent edge on the hand."

By adding some the above to your playing arsenal, you will be improving your chances of winning.

CHAPTER 5

Any Questions?

Question: *What is the average winning hand in blackjack for the player?*
Answer: Approximately 18.8. Many players think the 18 is a strong hand. It isn't. It is a long-term loser.

Question: *How often does the dealer get a blackjack when he has an ace showing? How often will the dealer get a blackjack overall?*
Answer: Approximately 32 percent of the time the dealer will get a blackjack with an ace as his up-card. The dealer (and the player) will get a blackjack approximately five percent of the time. Slightly more black-jacks are dealt at single-deck than at multiple-deck games.

Question: *How often will the dealer bust with various up-cards?*
Answer: It turns out that the key to knowing whether the dealer is going to bust is there in front of you on every hand.

So, let's look at the big picture first, and let me ask you this: How many times, say in every seven hands, do you think that the dealer will bust? Once? Twice? Maybe four times? The answer is twice. Yes, on average the dealer is going to bust about two times in every seven hands, which equates to about 29 percent of the time. That's an interesting statistic, but it doesn't really help us when we are staring at a dealer's 7 up-card while we are holding a 10-6 and deciding how to play the hand.

Fortunately for blackjack players, there happens to be a correlation between (don't be shocked now) the dealer's up-card and the percent of the time she will bust. The mathematicians have done all the calculations, and here are the facts.

Dealer's Up-card	2	3	4	5	6	7	8	9	10	Ace
Chance of Busting	35%	37%	40%	42%	42%	26%	24%	23%	23%	17%

Glance from left to right at the dealer's bust percentages in the table, and you'll see the significant drop between a dealer's 6 and 7 up-card. The numbers clearly show that the dealer's chance of busting is *greater* when she has a small up-card (2 though 6), and *less* when her up-card is a big card of 7 through ace.

The reason the dealer busts more often when she has a small up-card is because her initial two-card hand will be less than 17, and by the house rules, she must hit—with the one exception being if the rules specify that she stands on Soft 17. As long as the dealer has to hit in order to get to 17 to 21, there is a good chance that she will bust.

On the other hand, when the dealer shows a 7 through ace up-card, her chance of having an initial two-card pat hand of 17 to 21 is much better, because all she needs is a 10-valued card in the hole—and there are 16 of them per deck, or approximately 30 percent of the cards.

It is no accident that the basic blackjack playing strategy diverges below and above the dealer's up-card of 6 and 7. You generally will stand when you have a stiff hand (12 through 16) and the dealer shows a small up-card because, according to the above percentages, the dealer's chance of busting is relatively high. Likewise, we tend to double and split more often when the dealer shows a small up-card partly because her chance of busting increases.

On the other hand, when the dealer shows a 7 through ace and has less chance of busting and a greater chance of making a pat 17 through 21, we don't stand on stiff hands. In fact, risky as it sounds, the best play to make is to hit your stiff hand until you achieve a total of 17 through 21 (or bust out trying).

In today's world, more casinos are implementing the H17 rule, meaning their dealers no longer stand on Soft 17 (S17) but hit that hand. When the rules specify H17, the dealer's chance of busting when she has a 6 and ace up-card will increase. With a 6, it increases from 42 to nearly 44 percent, and with the ace, it increases from 17 to 20 percent. Because the dealer busts more often, this would appear to make an H17 game better for players than an S17 game. Not so. When the dealer hits her Soft 17 hand and doesn't bust, she will now improve her Soft 17 and achieve a final hand of 18 through 21 more often than with S17, and that is not good news for players. In fact, the latter more than compensates for the increase in the dealer's bust percentage, resulting in a net increase in the house edge against players of about 0.2 percent (20 cents per $100 wagered) when casinos implement the H17 rule.

Now that you have some idea of the chance that the dealer will bust by just looking at her up-card, you will better understand why the basic playing strategy tells you to hit some hands and stand on others. In short, it's all in the math.

Question: *What are the top five winning two-card hands for the player?*
Answer: If the player is betting $100, here are the top five winning two-card hands in terms of money made:
1. Ace-10 (blackjack): plus $144
2. Any 20: plus $58
3. Any 19: plus $27
4. Any 11: plus $18
5. Pair of Aces: plus $16

Question: *What are the five worst two-card hands for the player?*
Answer: If the player is betting $100, here is the losing expectation for the five worst two-card hands:
1. Any 16: minus $42
2. Any 15: minus $40
3. Any 14: minus $37
4. Any 13: minus $35
5. Any 12: minus $32

Question: *How often will the player bust on various hands he must hit?*
Answer: Assuming the use of a proper Basic Strategy, the player will bust at the following rate for these various hands:

Player Hand	Bust Rate
16	61 percent
15	59 percent
14	56 percent
13	52 percent
12	48 percent

Question: *How often will a player bust overall?*
Answer: A player will bust about 17 percent of the time.

Question: *What is the breakdown on how many hands a dealer wins, how many hands a player wins, and how many hands are ties?*
Answer: To make it easy to remember, I am eliminating fractions. The dealer will win about 48 percent of the time, the player will win about 44 percent of the time, and 8 percent of the hands will be pushes (ties).

Question: *If the dealer wins so much more, how is blackjack such a close game between the Basic Strategy player and the house?*
Answer: Because of the 3-to-2 payoff on a blackjack and the ability to double down and split pairs, the players win some hands with more money on them and obviously win a nice payoff for their blackjacks. That makes the game close. Also, that is why you don't want to play those 6-to-5 blackjack games!

CHAPTER 6

Prepare to Beat the House

For most blackjack players, card counting just isn't in their cards. It's hard to keep a traditional count accurately, with the constant adding and subtracting and multiplying and dividing, and betting properly, hand after hand, round after round. That's why the casinos have actually benefited from the card-counting revolution, because most of the would-be revolutionaries have died on the felt of battle. Although card counting has been around for decades, the success stories are few and far between.

The failure stories dominate. The success stories have books and movies written about them because they are so rare.

And so it has remained. A scant few thousand card counters out of about 10 million current blackjack players beat the game, and the rest of the blackjack players, even those who are smart players playing perfect Basic Strategy, are losers. Casino executives are very happy about that, too.

So it has remained.

Until *now*, that is.

Until Dan Pronovost, the skinny genius, arrived on the scene and revealed three years of his intense research, until the number 2.7's dimensions were fully understood.

Fix your mind on that number: 2.7 (*two-point-seven*). It is the magic behind the simplest method ever devised to get an edge over the game of blackjack. Remember this too—the average number of cards each player gets is 2.7.

All current card-counting systems use some form of the count-the-low-cards/count-the-high-cards method, then divide and/or multiply, then figure your edge and usually bet that percent of your bankroll. *But not Speed Count.* Of the 2.7 cards that each player gets, on average one will be a small card, or a card less than 7. Dan Pronovost asked himself this question: "Is it possible that a player could keep track of the small cards only—and to heck with the big cards?"

Pronovost created Speed Count, a method for getting a nice healthy edge at blackjack without any of the overwhelming burdens of the traditional card-counting systems. In fact, Speed Count is so simple that players who failed miserably at traditional card counting will probably have no trouble learning this in a staggeringly short period of time. It's that easy.

Dan did billions of computer simulations of the Speed Count and knew that it was an advantage-play method that no one had ever thought of before. It sure worked on the computer. But how easy would it really be to use in the casinos? After all, that is the true test of any advantage-play method—does it work in the real casino wars, or is it just a fancy computer-generated strategy?

So a team of us went into the casinos to see if this method was as easy as it seemed. It was. In fact, it was even easier than it seemed. For six months the three of us played Speed Count in the casinos of Nevada, New Jersey, Mississippi, and the Midwest. Dan played it in Canada, making his way to the many casinos on his trusty dogsled. Henry Tamburin and I played it in single-deck games, double-deck games, six-deck games, and eight-deck games.

The method worked—to perfection. It was easy to play. It required almost no mental energy. You could play Speed Count and talk to the pit bosses and the floor people. You could watch the ballgames on the televisions in the casinos. *You could look like a normal player. In fact, even better!—you could look really stupid while playing it.*

All the things card counters do as they are counting the cards, we didn't have to do. We could look like your average idiot, the average ploppy—which in a casino is a good thing. Idiots are loved in casinos.

Ploppies are worshipped. Smart players are hated. Card counters are despised. But Speed Count doesn't operate at all like those old traditional card-counting systems, so while card counters are busy sucking up all the big and little cards as they come out of the shoe or deck, a Speed Counter can sip his drink and watch television or the waitress or the waiter or all three!

Speed Count will not give you the same kind of edge as you get with the Hi-Lo counting system or many of the other, even harder traditional card-counting systems, but so what? If you tried Hi-Lo and failed to be able to do it, what do you care that your edge is somewhat smaller now that you finally have an edge? You work much harder with traditional counting systems. Why not use one that is so much easier to learn and accurately play?

Players can get tired playing Hi-Lo or other traditional counting systems for a few hours at a time, and they make mistakes that damage their edge. Speed Count was easy, it worked, and it gave us a nice edge at the game. It doesn't get much better than that.

I had been playing Hi-Lo for two decades, and I realized it was time to sit back, light up a grossly expensive cigar (I actually don't smoke), drink a fine glass of Belvedere vodka, and get an edge over the house without the work I used to do with Hi-Lo. Speed Count was wonderful for that. In fact, I could play longer and still make the kind of money I was making playing shorter sessions of Hi-Lo. I would also get a lot more in comps. The good life was here for my team and me!

Yes, some of the pompous old guard will snort and sniff at what good old Dan Pronovost has discovered. They will say things like, "Uh, uhm, ooo, eee, Hi-Lo is better, ee, oww, ooo." But do you care that they think you should be playing a card-counting method that most people can't learn to use—in short, why do they recommend systems that only a teeny-weeny fraction of the blackjack players can play? I'll answer for you—their egos are tied up in the idea that only the elite should get an edge at the game, and, of course, they consider themselves this elite.

Now, if you have tried to count the traditional way and have failed or found it a real boring burden, it doesn't matter what the old guard thinks. For you, the true blackjack savior has arrived, and it's Speed Count, despite what the self-styled elite pontificate.

Speed Count coupled with a brand-new Basic Strategy (called OBS for *Optimum Basic Strategy*), attached to our simple insurance strategies, our simple game-exit strategies, and our simple betting strategies will allow you to do to the casinos what they do to almost everyone else. And it is all EASY. I capitalized easy because it is all EASY!

Speed Count is new. Speed Count is revolutionary. Speed Count works. And Speed Count is easy to learn and easy to use. It gives you a good edge over the casino that you will be able to exploit.

The new OBS will increase the edge Speed Count gives us, as will our insurance and exit strategies.

Glorious! Spectacular! (Hey, don't say anything to the old guard but... "Welcome to the new elite!")

CHAPTER 7

How Speed Count Works

ecause every player and the dealer will receive an average of 2.7 cards per hand, one of which will be a small card, to perform Speed Count, you add up the small cards that have come out (the small cards are 2, 3, 4, 5, and 6), and you subtract the number of completed hands (including the dealer's hand) from the total.

You do not do the adding and subtracting while the hands are being played. You are not interested in the cards; you are interested in the hands, and the hands exist only when the player stops playing them.

And what is the total that you subtract these numbers from?

Okay, let us take a typical two-deck game first.

Dan Pronovost has determined through billions of computer simulations that the count for a double-deck game starts at 30. Let us say there are two players—you and a ploppy. You also have the dealer. That's *three hands* being played. So you will subtract three from the total after a round. If there is a split you will subtract four. If there are two splits you will subtract five. (Splits count as separate hands.)

Now the dealer deals out the cards: you get a 10 and a 2; the ploppy gets a 6 and 4; and the dealer shows a 6 as the up-card. So do you start counting right now?

No, you don't. No hand has been played.

Other card counters are busily counting right now, but you are doing nothing. You do not start counting because—I'll say this again—*no hands have been played*. I repeat, NO HANDS HAVE BEEN PLAYED. Now I usually don't like to use all caps, as that is considered yelling when you write on a message board on the Internet, but in Speed Count it is essential that you not count a small card until a hand has been played (any completed hand is considered "played," even hands swept off the board by a dealer blackjack). If I have to I will put that in caps again....

What makes Speed Count different from all counting strategies is the fact that you are adding small cards and subtracting them based on *the number of hands*—I repeat, *the number of hands*—so if a hand is not finished, there is no counting going on. Yes, that means if a small card should fall out of the dealer's hand and is then put in the discard rack—it is *not* counted, as that card does not relate to a player's hand. This is not traditional card counting. I repeat, this is *not* traditional card counting.

Okay, let's go around the table:

You stand on your 10 and 2 against the dealer's 6. Your hand is finished. The count is now 31—you started with 30 on the two-deck game, added one for your small card of 2, and so you now have a 31 count.

Now the ploppy has to play his hand. He doubles on his 6 and 4 and gets a 5. His hand is finished. There are three small cards now added to your 31 (6, 4, and 5), and the Speed Count is now at 34.

Finally the dealer turns over his hole card, a 10, and he has 16. He hits and busts with a 10. You add his small card (the 6) to the total of 34, and you now have 35.

Three hands were now played, so you subtract three from 35 and you get 32. That is your new count, 32, and that means you have an edge over the house. I'll explain in a little while how to bet with your edges, but for now, just get the picture:

1. You start the two-deck game at the count of 30.
2. When a hand is finished being played, you add all the small cards in that hand to the count of 30. In our example we got to 35 at the end of the round.
3. When all hands have been played, you subtract the number of hands from the total to arrive at your new count. In the above example, we subtracted three hands from 35 to arrive at 32.

That's it folks; that is Speed Count.

There are none of the mathematical gymnastics you have to do with traditional card counting. You add the small cards when a player's hand is finished; then you subtract the number of hands from the initial count. Bingo! You have your new count. Over 31, you have the edge. Under 31, the casino has the edge.

Let's try it again to make sure we have it down pat. We are still playing a two-deck game played face up. The count starts at 30. There are five people at the table this time—four players and the dealer. (Yes, the dealer's hand counts too! Please don't forget that.)

The dealer deals out the following:
Player One: 10:5
Player Two: 10:10
Player Three: 5:7
Player Four: 9:9
Dealer Up-card: 7

What is the count right now? *It is still 30 because no hands have been played.* This is the key ingredient—when the cards are being dealt out, you should be doing something other than looking at all the cards. When a hand is being played, then you look at the cards for that hand. This is a radical departure from traditional card counting. It makes you look like a regular player.

Now we play the hands.

Player One hits his 10:5 and busts with a 7. You add one to the count of 30 because Player One had a small card (the 5). The count is now 31.

Player Two stands on his 20. You add nothing to the count because Player Two did not have a small card. The count is still 31.

Player Three hits his 5:7 and gets a 9. You add one to the count as Player Three had a small card (a 5). The count is now 32.

Player Four stands on his 9:9. You add nothing to the count, because Player Four does not have a small card in his hand. The count is still 32.

The dealer turns over a 10 for a 10:7 and stands. You add nothing to the count because the dealer does not have a small card. The count is still 32.

There are five hands that have been played. You subtract five from 32, and you get 27. That is your new count. The house has the edge because the count is *less than* 31.

So now the next round begins, and your count is 27. So let's deal out some more cards:

Player One gets a 2:3

Player Two gets a 6:6

Player Three gets a 10:4

Player Four gets a 7:3

Dealer gets an up-card of 6

What is the count? It is 27! That is the count that started this round, and it is still the count, because no hands have been played. I repeat— **NO HANDS HAVE BEEN PLAYED.** (My wife, the beautiful A.P., is going to kill me for using bolds, caps, and italics so much.)

Let's play the hands.

Player One hits his 2:3 and gets a 5. He hits again and gets a 2. He now stands. He received four small cards (2, 3, 5, and 2), so you add four to 27, and the count is now 31.

Player Two splits his 6:6 against the dealer's up-card of 6. We have just added an *extra hand* to the game for this round. The best thing to do is subtract this hand *right now* so the count is now 30.

On the first 6, the player gets a 5; the player doubles and gets a 10. You now add two to the count, as the player received two small cards (6 and 5). The count is now 32. On the second hand of 6, the dealer gives the player a 9, and the player stands. You add one to the count, as the player had one small card (the 6). The count is now 33.

Player Three stands on his 10:4. You add one to the count, as he had a small card (the 4). The count is now 34.

Player Four doubles on his 7:3 and gets a 4. He now stands. Because two small cards came out (the 3 and 4), the count goes to 36.

The dealer turns over her hole card and has a 10 underneath. She hits her 10:6 and gets an 8, and busts. We add one to the count because the dealer had one small card (the 6). The count is now 37.

We subtract the five hands (four players and one dealer) from 37, and the count is now 32. Remember, on the split we subtracted the extra hand immediately. Splits will occur about 2 percent of the time, so just subtracting immediately will not confuse us when we do our end-of-the-round subtraction. Repeat: Subtract the split hand immediately.

Okay, you have just learned the essentials of the Speed Count. In a two-deck game, you start at 30. When you get to 31, you have an edge over the house; when you are under 31, the house has the edge over you. It is as simple as can be.

Number of Decks

Of course, not all games are double-deckers. Although the number *31* will indicate an edge at all games, the starting number for Speed Count will change based on the number of decks. Here's how to begin your Speed Count with various decks:

- The ultimate single-deck games with DAS (double after splits) and S17 (dealer standing on Soft 17): Speed Count begins at 31. (Yes, you have an edge off the top in this game—if you can find this game, that is.)
- Single-deck games (Inferior rules but *never* games that pay 6-to-5 for blackjacks): Speed Count begins at 30.
- All double-deck games: Speed Count begins at 30.
- All four-deck games: Speed Count begins at 29.
- All six-deck games: Speed Count begins at 27.
- All eight-deck games: Speed Count begins at 26.

Obviously, the rules of the game and the penetration of the game will determine how strong your edge is at 31—although 31 will always indicate an edge at *all* games. If the casino allows DAS, S17, resplits, and surrender, your 31 will be stronger than the 31 in a game where the dealer hits Soft 17 (H17), where you can't double after splits, and where you can't resplit or surrender. Still 31 is the magic number because, at that number, you get the best of the casino, regardless of the rules. As you head up the scale to 32, 33, 34, 35, and higher, your edge gets stronger and stronger over the casino.

The reverse is also true. At 30, the casino has an edge in all games. In good games (DAS, resplits, S17, and surrender) that edge is smaller than at bad games (no DAS, no resplits, H17, and no surrender). But no matter the rules, at 30 the edge favors the house. As you go down the scale to 29, 28, 27, 26, 25, and lower, the house edge becomes stronger and stronger over you.

Face-Up and Face-Down Games

Some new advantage-play blackjack players get themselves in a state of high anxiety because they think that games that are dealt face down—meaning you can't see the other players' cards until he or she busts or the dealer turns them over at the end—makes Speed Count harder to do. Nothing is further from the truth.

It doesn't matter that the cards are face down on the table. You aren't counting cards; you are *counting hands played* and adding small cards, and, again, the small cards are not counted until *the hand is played*. In face-down games, when a player busts, his cards are turned over. The dealer takes his money and then his cards. You have plenty of time to add the small cards when this happens.

At the end, when the dealer turns over his own cards, you add the small cards in his hand. Then the dealer goes from player to player, turning over the cards, seeing what the hand is, paying or taking the bets. That's when you add the small cards.

No dealer is so fast that you can't add the small cards. In a normal blackjack game, the hand is not quicker than the eye. The "hand faster than the eye" saying is only true in magic or cheating.

Face-up games are just a little more orderly, but, regardless, Speed Counting that face-down game is quite easy. Because most of the better games are dealt from double-decks, these are usually (although not always) dealt face down.

Why Such High Speed-Count Numbers?

Now, you might want to know why we use the number 31 and other numbers in that particular range for Speed Count. All the other count systems use much lower numbers and also negative numbers. There are two reasons for why we kept our numbers high.

1. Most fledgling card counters have difficulty mentally adding and subtracting positive and negative integers, which is required in most traditional card-counting systems. It's easy to add +4 to a +2 and get a +6. But what does +2 added to a -5 equal? How about adding -7 to a +3? To avoid having to deal with negative integers with Speed Count, the pivot point was set at 31, and the initial speed count (ISC) was set at 30 (single- and double-deck), 29 (four decks), 27

(six decks), and 26 (eight decks). Another benefit is that, regardless of the number of decks, players who use Speed Count know that the edge shifts from the house to the player as soon as the Speed Count increases to 31 or higher.

2. Sometimes you might be playing at the same table with another Speed Counter, which we'll talk about later in this book, and one of you loses the count. If you ask him what he thinks the weather in Alaska is right now, and he says, "I heard it was 33 degrees," well, you know where the Speed Count is. It is rare that normal counting systems ever get their counts into such high numbers, and the casino pits are not trained to hear those high numbers. Everything we have done with Speed Count is to make it react unlike all the other counting systems. We want you to be doing what other advantage blackjack players don't do. The casinos have trained themselves to hunt and destroy traditional card counters. Well, Speed Counters are not going to look much like those traditional counters. So we put our numbers higher partly for that purpose.

CHAPTER 8

Betting Your Count

When the edge favors the casino, you want to bet small (or not at all), but when the edge favors you, you want to bet big. An advantage player at blackjack has to get the money on the table when the game favors him. It's the only way to win in the long run. Getting the money on the table in "good" counts (also called "high" counts) makes up for the steady losses you get when the game favors the house. Let's look at two methods of betting at this game, conservative and aggressive.

I will use the word "units" in describing how to bet. Your unit can be $5, $10, $12.50, $20, $25, $100, $101, and so on. You determine what a unit is. The betting recommendations coming up are just that—recommendations. You can bet more if you want, although I would not recommend betting more in low "good" counts because your edge at 31 is small no matter what game you are playing.

Insurance

"Never take insurance!" That's a dictum given to Basic Strategy players, and for them it is a truism. For you, the truth lies elsewhere. The insurance bet can be a good thing for the Speed Counter when used properly. Thus, there will also be a number given at which insurance is a bet that gives you an edge. To insure properly, you must do the counting exactly as described. Some players like to flip the counting upside down and do the subtraction of the number of hands first, but that can get very confusing for the insurance decisions, which are based on the *past count* and not the future count. This technique for insurance is also quite different than what traditional card counters do in trying to exploit the insurance bet. Traditional card counters are very concerned with the cards that have just come out when the dealer shows an ace. Those of you playing Speed Count are not concerned with the cards that have just come out, because no hands have been played or completed.

Exit Strategies

The lower the Speed Count goes, the worse it is for the advantage-play Speed Counter. There are counts that you'd like to sit out at every game because the casino edge is ridiculously high, and we will indicate what these counts are as well. Now, you can sit out all the counts at this range or just some of them some of the time. Remember, you don't want the floor person or pit boss to notice that you sit out too many low counts, because that is a technique that card counters often use. Sitting out some of them is a good thing to do, though. You can go to the bathroom on one low count, get a cell-phone call on another low count (keep your phone off so it doesn't ring as you are pretending to talk into it), or just sit out a hand as players will sometimes do. Selecting when to sit out helps your edge increase over the game. Playing in the really low counts hurts your bankroll.

The Bottom Line

It is our opinion that if you use the conservative method of betting coming up, the casinos will have a very difficult time of getting a bead on the fact that you have an advantage. In fact, at 31 we find an edge over the house that the other card counters don't usually see. Therefore we are upping our bet before the traditional card counters will be upping their bets. As the counts go higher than 31, the traditional counting systems and Speed Count will reflect each other much more. But at 31, chances are that our bets will be increased and the traditional counter's bet might just be his initial low bet.

However, if you become a more aggressive bettor, especially those of you betting green, black, and purple (or higher) chips, the casino will scrutinize your play much more closely because you are jumping your bets considerably and the total amount of the money being wagered is rather large. If you use the super-aggressive strategies, you might find that some casinos might ask you not to play. Treading cautiously is a wise way to go—especially as you get the feel of what it is like to actually be playing a game that can beat the casinos, which you will be doing.

Playing for only 30 minutes to 45 minutes when you bet aggressively is the best advice we can give you. You don't want the casinos to get a good bead on you. Conservative bettors can probably play much longer in the same casino that aggressive players must hit and run.

Speed Count Betting for Different Games

Single-deck games with DAS (Double After Splits) and S17 (Dealer Standing on Soft 17): Speed Count Begins at 31.

Conservative:
At the start: Bet two units, since you have the edge
27 or under: Exit game
30 or under: Bet one unit
31: Bet two units
32 or higher: Bet three units
Insure your hand if the count is 33 or higher

Aggressive:
At the start: Bet two units, since you have the edge
27 or under: Exit game
30 or under: Bet one unit
31: Bet two units
32: Bet three units
33: Bet four units
34: Bet five units
35: Bet six units
Insure your hand if the count is 33 or higher

Super Aggressive:
At the start: Bet three units, since you have the edge
27 or under: Exit game
30 or under: Bet one unit
31: Bet three units

32: Bet four units

33: Spread to two hands and bet four units on each hand

34: Stay at two hands and bet five units on each hand

35: Stay at two hands and bet six units on each hand

Insure your hand if the count is 33 or higher

Single-Deck Games (Inferior Rules): Speed Count begins at 30.

Conservative:

At the start: Bet one unit, as the casino has the edge.

27 or under: Exit game

30 or under: Bet one unit

31: Bet two units

32 or higher: Bet three units

Insure your hand if the count is 33 or higher

Aggressive:

At the start: Bet one unit, as the casino has the edge.

27 or under: Exit game

30 or under: Bet one unit

31: Bet two units

32: Bet three units

33: Bet four units

34: Bet five units

35: Bet six units

Insure your hand if the count is 33 or higher

Super Aggressive:

At the start: Bet one unit, as the casino has the edge.

27 or under: Exit game

30 or under: Bet one unit

31: Bet three units

32: Bet four units

33: Spread to two hands and bet four units on each hand

34: Stay at two hands and bet five units on each hand

35: Stay at two hands and bet six units on each hand

Insure your hand if the count is 33 or higher

Double-Deck Games (All Rules): Speed Count begins at 30.

Conservative:
At the start: Bet one unit, as the casino has the edge.
26 or under: Exit game
30 or under: Bet one unit
31: Bet two units
32 or higher: Bet four units
Insure your hand if the count is 34 or higher

Aggressive:
At the start: Bet one unit, as the casino has the edge.
26 or under: Exit game
30 or under: Bet one unit
31: Bet two units
32: Bet four units
33: Bet six units
34: Bet eight units
Insure your hand if the count is 34 or higher

Super Aggressive:
At the start: Bet one unit, as the casino has the edge.
26 or under: Exit game
30 or under: Bet one unit
31: Bet two units
32: Bet four units
33: Spread to two hands and bet four units on each hand
34: Stay at two hands and bet six units on each hand
35: Stay at two hands and bet eight units on each hand
Insure your hand if the count is 34 or higher

Four Deck Games (All Rules): Speed Count begins at 29.

Conservative:
At the start: Bet one unit, as the casino has the edge.
23 or under: Exit game
30 or under: Bet one unit
31: Bet two units

32: Bet three units

33: Bet four units

34: Bet five units

Insure your hand if the count is 37 or higher.

Aggressive:

At the start: Bet one unit, as the casino has the edge.

23 or under: Exit game

30 or under: Bet one unit

31: Bet two units

32: Bet four units

33: Bet six units

34: Bet eight units

Insure your hand if the count is 37 or higher.

Super Aggressive:

At the start: Bet one unit, as the casino has the edge.

23 or under: Exit game

30 or under: Bet one unit

31: Bet two units

32: Bet four units

33: Spread to two hands and bet four units on each hand

34: Stay at two hands and bet six units on each hand

35: Stay at two hands and bet eight units on each hand

36: Stay at two hands and bet 10 units on each hand

Insure your hand if the count is 37 or higher.

Six-Deck Games (All Rules): Speed Count begins at 27.

Conservative:

At the start: Bet one unit, as the casino has the edge.

21 or under: Exit game

30 or under: Bet one unit

31: Bet two units

32: Bet four units

33: Bet eight units

Insure your hand if the count is 38 or higher

Aggressive:

At the start: Bet one unit, as the casino has the edge.

21 or under: Exit game

30 or under: Bet one unit

31: Bet two units

32: Bet four units

33: Bet eight units

34: Bet 10 units

35: Bet 12 units

Insure your hand if the count is 38 or higher

Super Aggressive:

At the start: Bet one unit, as the casino has the edge.

21 or under: Exit game

30 or under: Bet one unit

31: Bet two units

32: Bet four units

33: Bet eight units

34: Bet 10 units

35: Bet two hands of 10 units each

36: Bet two hands of 12 units each

37: Bet two hands of 15 units each

Insure your hand if the count is 38 or higher

Eight-Deck Games (All Rules): Speed Count begins at 26.

Conservative:

At the start: Bet one unit, as the casino has the edge.

20 or under: Exit game

30 or under: Bet one unit

31: Bet two units

32: Bet four units

33: Bet six units

34: Bet eight units

35: Bet 10 units

Insure your hand if the count is 40 or higher

Aggressive:

At the start: Bet one unit, as the casino has the edge.

20 or under: Exit game

30 or under: Bet one unit

31: Bet two units

32: Bet four units

33: Bet eight units

34: Bet 12 units

35: Bet 15 units

Insure your hand if the count is 40 or higher

Super Aggressive:

At the start: Bet one unit, as the casino has the edge.

20 or under: Exit game

30 or under: Bet one unit

31: Bet two units

32: Bet four units

33: Bet eight units

34: Bet 12 units

35: Bet two hands of 12 units on each hand

36: Bet two hands of 15 units on each hand

37: Bet two hands of 20 units on each hand

Insure your hand if the count is 40 or higher

A word of caution is warranted here. Using the super-aggressive strategies will bring a lot of attention to you, so if you feel this is the method of play you'd like to use, then you mustn't stay more than a half-hour in the game before moving on. Even though Speed Count is something new and revolutionary, jumping your bets into the stratosphere will bring attention to you.

CHAPTER 9

About This and About That

Okay, this is the chapter that is going to drive the elite's propeller hats crazy, as I am going to talk about things using the words "about," "in general," "around," and "approximately." Which means there aren't going to be decimal places to the fortieth *entity* (*my* math word). Instead I want to give you an idea of how strong Speed Count is without also giving you a severe headache in the bargain.

However, if your pens are now frothing in your pocket protectors, relax, because Dan Pronovost, your new deity, has reams of *decimalized* information at the end of the book that you can devour the way he devours chocolate cream pies. He has gone nuts with math for you and computer simulations and everything that makes life worth living for those who have become one with their slide rules (are those used anymore?) and computers.

Speed Count and Basic Strategy

A Basic Strategy player using one of the casino Basic Strategy cards or one of the Basic Strategies from any good blackjack book will be playing against about ½-percent house edge. That means he will lose around 50 cents for every $100 he bets.

If you are a $10 Basic Strategy player, you will lose approximately $5 per hour, assuming you will be playing around 100 hands per hour. Losing

$5 per hour is not so outrageous considering a Megabucks slot player can lose around $400 per hour pumping in $3 per spin.

Still, Basic Strategy players are losers.

A *conservative* $10 Speed Counter will win about $9 per hour. Chew on that! You can *lose* $5 per hour as a Basic Strategy player or you can *win* $9 per hour as a Speed Counter. Hmmm. Which do you want to do?

Now, obviously, because you are raising your bets in good counts, the average bet of a Speed Counter is higher than the average bet of the Basic Strategy player, but those bets are raised only when you have the edge—not when the casino has the edge.

If you bet certain amounts:

Amount Wagered As Base Bet	Basic Strategy LOSS per Hour	Speed Count WIN per Hour
$10	-$5	+$9
$15	-$7.50	+$13.50
$20	-$10	+$18
$25	-$12.50	+$22.50
$50	-$25	+$45
$100	-$50	+$90
$200	-$100	+$180
$500	-$250	+$450

The Speed Counter clearly wins a nice amount of money per hour using a conservative approach. He will win even more using more aggressive approaches, as Dan Pronovost discusses later.

Average Bets

A $10 Speed Counter does not have an average bet of $10. In fact, because he is raising his bets in good counts and also doubling and splitting in all counts, his average bet per hand is approximately $21. The Basic Strategy player is actually betting about $12 per hour because of splits and double-downs.

Although average bet size is interesting for bankroll sizing, it is not something that should scare you. In fact, your comps are going to go up because your average bet has gone up. If you wish to be a conservative player, your bankroll does not have to be massive to allow you to play with the confidence that you won't get wiped out if a bad streak hits you. And by the way, you will get hit with bad streaks. We all do.

Maybe I should pause here to tell you about the fact that even as an advantage player you can lose—and lose and lose. Yes, your overall expectation will be positive, but like even the best fighters who ever lived, you are going to take some shots to the head. Get used to that idea. You will win in the long run, but you can (and will) take your lumps even as an advantage player.

Here's a story to let you know what you can experience:

Dominator: *We taught John the Speed Count in a private Golden Touch Blackjack class, and he was adept at it within a half hour. We also taught him Optimum Basic Strategy and other techniques to protect him against casino heat. He went to the casinos the very next week and won $200,000 in three days. He was in heaven, as he had lost millions in his blackjack-playing career up to that time.*

We all cautioned John that he was experiencing a hot streak, what the math boys call a positive fluctuation, and that he could expect a negative fluctuation too. We couldn't predict when it would happen, but we could predict that it would happen—it is always going to happen. You don't win every session even when you have the edge, because that edge is tiny.

When John revisited the casinos a few weeks later, he hit the wall. He lost three days in a row, sums of $40,000, $30,000, and $30,000. He was crestfallen. He was disheartened. He said he was losing confidence in the Speed Count, that maybe it didn't work and he should go back to playing the way he used to.

The way he used to play lost him millions! But when you get discouraged, you tend to return to what brought you to the Speed Count in the first place—lousy losing strategies!

John was completely wrong on this—obviously. He had won $200,000 and lost $100,000. The Speed Count was working fine. He was also in a very short run. Thankfully, John had a small winning streak and regained *his confidence in the Speed Count. But those losing days had thrown him. Let me say this for everyone to hear:* **people can have losing sessions, days, weeks, and maybe even months** *despite the fact that they have the edge.*

Frank once lost 20 hands in a row. Both Henry Tamburin and I were at the same table with him when this happened. I've gone days where I can't buy a win. So has Henry. So has Dan. It is the nature of the game for you to have ups and downs, but over time your ups will win out if you play properly. Don't panic if you lose. You have the edge, but that edge is small. As Frank says, you will have to get used to the fact that you will be taking some lumps. But a Basic Strategy player takes many more lumps and is a loser in the end. That's the big difference. A Speed Counter is a winner; all the others are losers. When a bad streak occurs, say that in your mind: I am a winner. I will play perfectly. I am a winner. *Don't play scared.*

What Is My Edge?

Dan Pronovost has reams of information about the whole range of edges that you can get with Speed Count at the various games using conservative and aggressive strategies. But some rules of thumb apply, and you should know these. You don't have to memorize Dan's charts in Chapter 18, but you should acquaint yourself with certain facts about the edge at blackjack.

The edge with Speed Count can go from one-tenth of a percent (you win a dime for every $100 you wager) to 1.5 percent (you win $1.50 for every $100 you wager). Of course, to get that 1.5 percent, you must be a super-aggressive player, something that is really not recommended for most of you, and you must be playing games with deep penetration and great rules.

At the bottom end, the one-tenth of a percent, are games with six players and horrible rules with no DAS and dealers hitting Soft 17. A conservative strategy at this game yields a very small return. (As bad as it is, it is still better than being a Basic Strategy player and much better than being a ploppy.)

In fact, you will probably be playing games and strategies somewhere between these two extremes. Your edge will probably be around one-half percent, give or take a tenth of a percent. This is damn good, considering the effort needed to attain this edge is very small.

How Often Will I Hit Various Counts?
Six Decks/DAS/S17/75 percent Penetration/4 Players

Speed Count	Frequency of Appearance	Expectation Percent
14	0.14	-3.74
15	0.23	-3.61
16	0.37	-3.05
17	0.57	-2.85
18	0.87	-2.60
19	1.28	-2.44
20	1.83	-1.97
21	2.54	-1.83
22	3.43	-1.49
23	4.52	-1.19
24	5.76	-1.02
25	6.98	-0.80
26	7.93	-0.58
27	14.03	-0.42
28	8.25	-0.29
29	7.69	-0.14
30	6.87	0.05
31	5.92	0.16
32	4.96	0.43
33	4.05	0.56
34	3.21	0.76
35	2.48	0.92
36	1.86	1.27
37	1.35	1.49
38	0.95	1.61
39	0.65	1.69

Speed Count	Frequency of Appearance	Expectation Percent
40	0.43	2.01
41	0.28	1.98
42	0.17	2.36
43	0.10	2.57
44	0.06	2.87
45	0.03	2.91
46	0.02	3.05
47	0.01	2.28

Two Decks/DAS/S17/67 Percent Penetration/4 Players

Speed Count	Frequency of Appearance	Expectation Percent
14	0.00	-100.00
15	0.00	-68.18
16	0.00	-22.61
17	0.00	-5.48
18	0.00	-10.61
19	0.01	-9.83
20	0.03	-7.41
21	0.07	-7.41
22	0.19	-6.15
23	0.46	-5.28
24	1.00	-4.33
25	2.02	-3.39
26	3.74	-2.56
27	6.24	-1.91
28	9.07	-1.27
29	11.31	-0.67
30	29.99	-0.18
31	11.11	0.35
32	9.00	0.84

Speed Count	Frequency of Appearance	Expectation Percent
33	6.50	1.31
34	4.22	1.72
35	2.50	2.14
36	1.35	2.53
37	0.67	2.72
38	0.31	2.93
39	0.13	3.30
40	0.05	3.75
41	0.02	3.92
42	0.01	3.98
43	0.00	2.06
44	0.00	5.81
45	0.00	16.67
46	0.00	-35.71
47	0.00	-100.00

Good Games and Bad Games

I wrote a sentence more than two decades ago, but it bears rewriting: *Not all blackjack games are created equal.* Some games are good, some games are bad, and many games are inbetween those extremes. There are two ingredients that determine whether a game is good or bad: the rules of the game and the penetration—with penetration being the stronger element of the two.

So what is penetration? Take a deck of 52 cards, and take 26 out of play. That is penetration of 50 percent. It's poor penetration. Take a deck of cards and take 13 out of play. That is penetration of 75 percent. That is good penetration.

The rule of penetration applies to all blackjack games—the deeper the penetration the better it is for you. The more cards you get to play, the better it is for you. If the penetration is 75 percent or above, that is good; but if the penetration is hovering near 50 percent, that is not so good. Can you win at games where the penetration is 50 percent? Yes, there are many games that you can beat where the penetration is 50 percent, but your edge at these games is smaller than the edge you would get with that exact same game in terms of rules but with 75 percent penetration.

Most single-deck games have shallow penetration, as casinos are paranoid about card counters beating their most vulnerable games. In the old days you could find many casinos that dealt out 75 percent of a single-deck game. Today those games are rare, and 50 percent penetration is extant among the single-deckers.

Most double-deck games that are playable have penetration of about 60 to 66 percent, although you can find double-deck games with 75 percent or more penetration if you look for them.

While four-deck games are not the norm in casinos, as most casinos jump to six-deck games, the casinos that offer four-deckers will usually give penetration of between 60 percent and 75 percent.

On six-deck and eight-deck games, the penetration is usually 66 to 75 percent. Many casinos offer excellent six-deck games with penetration of 83 percent (one deck cut out of play), and these would be the preferred games in this variety. With both six-deck and eight-deck games, you have to practice patience, as the shoe will rarely go positive. There will be long stretches where you will be betting your minimum number of units. If you don't have patience or if your inner gambler eggs you to increase your bet when you don't have the edge, you will again belong to the loser group—the casino's favorite people! Single-deck and double-deck games are more explosive, as the counts vary wildly. But those big-shoe games are slow movers. So patience is the key for them.

Let's see how penetration affects your edge at a typical two-deck game and a typical six-deck game with four players at the table. We are using the conservative strategy for these charts. You can DAS, and the dealer stands on Soft 17.

Penetration

Two-Deck Game	Your Edge	Percentage Difference
5/6	0.66 percent	
3/4	0.55 percent	17 percent
2/3	0.46 percent	30 percent
1/2	0.31 percent	54 percent

Penetration

Six-Deck Game	Your Edge	Percentage Difference
5/6	0.48 percent	
3/4	0.37 percent	23 percent
2/3	0.30 percent	38 percent
1/2	0.16 percent	67 percent

While you still have an edge at both games when 50 percent of the cards are kept out of play, that edge is much, much smaller than the edge you get at five-sixths or three-fourths penetration. Although both the two- and six-deck games are beatable even with a 50 percent cut, your hourly win rate is reduced markedly if you play these games.

Good Rules

The next ingredient in good games is good rules. Here is a list of the good rules:

- Blackjack pays 3-to-2
- Insurance offered at 2-to-1 (insurance is good for Speed Counters)
- Double down on any first two cards
- Doubling down on soft hands
- Split any pairs
- Resplit any pairs
- Double down after pair splitting
- Split aces more than once
- Surrender
- Dealer stands on Soft 17 (S17)
- Entering game allowed mid-shoe

Bad Rules

Here are the bad rules:

- Blackjack pays 6-to-5
- No doubling down on any first two cards
- Doubling only on 10 or 11
- No doubling down on soft hands
- No pair splitting
- No resplitting of pairs
- No doubling down allowed after splits
- Dealer hits Soft 17 (H17)
- No mid-shoe entry allowed

Games where blackjack pays 6-to-5 cannot be beaten and should be avoided. This is a rule that devours players' bankrolls. If you bet $10 and get a blackjack, at a normal game you get paid $15 for your $10 wager. At the 6-to-5 games, you get paid $12 for a blackjack. The casino keeps the other $3! Never, never, NEVER play games where the house pays 6-to-5 for blackjacks.

You will find that many casinos have some good rules and some bad rules on the very same game. You might be able to double down on any first two cards, split and resplit, and double down after splits. That's good. However, the game has the dealer hitting his Soft 17s. That's bad. You try to get as many good rules as you can.

Given a deeply penetrated game with mediocre rules or a game that is poorly penetrated with good rules, you should opt for the deeply penetrated one. Recheck the penetration charts and see how powerful the element of penetration is. The deeper you go into the cards, the better your chance to hammer the casinos.

Those Infernal Shuffle Machines

There are two types of shuffling machines—one good, one bad. The good ones are those that shuffle the decks so that a new shoe is ready immediately without the dealer having to spend time shuffling the decks by hand. This makes the game faster for you, and fast is good, because you have the edge. The more decisions you play the better it is for you in the long run.

The bad machines are called "continuous-shuffle machines." There are no new shoes. There are no new rounds. The machine keeps shuffling the cards—endlessly. When a round is finished, the dealer dumps the played cards into the machine, which just shuffles them into the pack. There is no way to get an edge on continuous-shuffling machines and, like those 6-to-5 blackjack games, all games using such machines must be avoided.

CHAPTER 10

I Want You to Be Stupid

When you were in school, the stupid kids wanted everyone else to be as stupid as they were. They had this thing about freely sharing their idiocy. In fact, even if you didn't want to share in their stupidity and idiocy, they kind of made you because they disrupted classes, acted like fools in the hallways and cafeteria, and picked on people. Bullies were generally stupid. The stupid kids were hard to escape, and they seemed to be everywhere. Today you see them driving like nuts on the various roadways of America, but unless you are a teacher, you really don't have to react to the stupid kids, who are as abundant today as they have always been.

As an adult you are free to hang out only with adults who meet your intellectual and emotional needs. That's a good thing. Of course, if you are a teacher...my prayers are with you!

The smart kids, on the other hand, really did not try to make anyone else smart; they just went about the singular business of getting a good education and, for most of them, becoming successful in life. For some peculiar reason, secular evangelism among the young is reserved for the boneheads and not the brains.

Dominator, Henry, Dan, and I are glad that you are smart. We are glad that you have decided to become an advantage player at blackjack and that you are reading this book to build a solid foundation with our Golden Touch methods of advantage play.

Yes, it's great to be smart! Rejoice! Be happy! Big smile now! In the real world, smart is good. Unfortunately, stupid is widespread; smart is rare.

Now forget all about the fact that you are smart, because right now I want you to recall the jerks you went to high school with. Dig into your memory banks and look into their dull faces, their lackluster eyes; see their beetle brows. We want you to become as stupid as they were (and probably still are), because the casinos are like high schools with neon—they are dominated by the dopes. From slot machine to high-roller executive suite, stupidity is rewarded in the casinos. Smart players are despised; dopes are lionized.

The advice I am going to give you in this chapter will make you appear to be a dope, a dullard, a moron—a ploppy of immense magnitude and unimportance. Start drooling! Indeed, if you can learn to drool while you play, that would be very helpful, as it would make you look like a complete cretin and also make other players avoid playing at the same table with you—which is a very good thing for an advantage player. The fewer the players at the table with you, the better it is for you.

Now, the advice that is coming is good advice—and it will help you maintain a nice edge over the house and give you the appearance that you are not one of the swiftest of the bunch.

Where to Sit

Think quickly—which is the best seat to be at on a blackjack table? If you know anything about traditional card counting, you will snap out, "Third base!" That's the position that is last to get his cards. For card counters, third base is the best position. But for Speed Counters, third base is not the best position to be at—first base is the best position. You want to get your hand first. Thus first base allows you to play your hand and spend the rest of the time adding the small cards without worrying about figuring out your hand and having two numbers in your head—the hand and Speed Count.

The casino pit people are trained to suspect competent players at third base of being card counters. If you play at first base, especially if only you and one or two players are at the table, you don't look very suspicious. You benefit when you use Speed Count because your best position at the table makes you appear to be just another ploppy.

Don't Watch the Cards as the Dealer Deals

I mentioned this before, but it bears repeating—do not watch the cards as they are being dealt out. You can watch your own hand, that's normal, but ignore all the other hands. Talk to the floor person when the dealer is dealing. Henry Tamburin has a way of being so boring when he talks to the floor person that these characters flee him as if he has a plague—which he does, the plague of ploppiness. Although the casinos love the stupid people, individual casino people don't want to have long conversations with the ploppy brigades. That stands to reason; after all, who wants to talk to stupid people? You had to do that in high school.

Don't Add Up Other Players' or the Dealer's Hands

The Speed Count has just gone to 24, and you are adding up the dealer's hand. She has a 14 and takes a hit, gets an 8 for a 22. Hooray, she busted with 22! Uh, what's the count? Hmmm? Is it 22 or something else? Damn, I lost it adding up the dealer's hand!

Or I lost it adding up another player's hand.

So why are you adding up their totals? Does it help you play your hand? No, it doesn't. Does it help you keep the Speed Count? No it doesn't. Does it do any good at all? No, it doesn't. The totals of the hands of other players and the dealer are irrelevant to you. There is only one number you should be keeping in your head, and that number is the Speed Count.

When hands are finished, you don't care what total the player has or if the player busted or if the player plays "Jingle Bells" on his toes—you just want to know what the Speed Count is based on the small cards that have appeared as the hands go by. Adding up the hands of the other players is a waste of time and usually a very confusing waste of time. Let the other players add their own hands, and let the dealer add her own hand, too. You just keep the count and then do that final subtraction at the end of the round.

When the count is in your head, you don't want any other numbers interfering with it. Almost all other players are busy adding other players' and the dealer's hands. Good. Let them. You are so stupid you don't even care what the other players get on their hands. How's that? You don't even care what the dealer gets on her hand. The hell with the hands!

Just keep the Speed Count. Follow this advice, and it serves a dual purpose. You keep the count better, and you look like a real nut because you don't seem all that interested in what's going on in the game that you're risking money at.

Henry Tamburin: *It's no surprise that casinos love stupid players. To give the perception that I am a stupid player, I will sometimes make a few faux pas in procedures that will illicit a rebuke from the dealer. In hand-held games I might pick up both initial cards dealt to me with two hands or not turn over my cards when I double down. In face-down games, separating your cards during a pair split will often label you as a clueless player. How you place your chips in the betting circle also gives you an opportunity to play stupid. Put a higher-denomination chip on top of smaller denomination chip, and the dealer and fellow players will shake their heads. Better yet, when the dealer places your winning chips next to your original chips, leave them in the betting circle for the next hand.*

When it comes your turn to cut the deck after a shuffle, position the cut card three or four cards from the top or bottom of the deck(s). I also have my trusty strategy card in my hand or place it on the layout in full view of everyone (especially the floor person). I will, on occasion, give a perplexed look when dealt a "tough" hand and ask my fellow players or the dealer for advice on how to play it. Better yet, if the floor supervisor is at the table, I'll ask him by name, "Joe, what does the book say to play this hand?" Do that two different times with the same floor supervisor, and you'll never see him again at your table.

Clueless players seem to think blackjack is a team sport while they have fun losing their money. So I join in their fun by congratulating the anchor player when his smart play "saved the table," or I'll root loudly for the dealer's draw card to be a bust card when she has to draw with a stiff hand. When the dealer breaks, I cheer and clap just like my fellow players do. I'll also commiserate with a fellow player when he gets a bad draw and loses his hand. I'll also piss and moan loudly when I lose a hand due to a miracle draw by the dealer and state loudly, "Sue, you are killing me!"

Sitting out a few hands when the count goes south also gives me the opportunity to "help" my fellow players' fortunes by smartly saying, "I'm going to sit out a few hands to change the flow of the cards." Of course using the OBS card has several plays different from what a normal Basic Strategy player would do, so it sometimes brings a response from the dealer along the lines of, "Are you sure you want to stand on that hand?" My comeback is, "That's what my strategy card says to do, and I got it from my brother-in-law, and he told me he never loses."

To reach the pinnacle of stupidity, when the floor supervisor is within earshot I often make a comment after losing a few consecutive hands such as, "I can never win at this game. I guess I'm just not lucky with cards."

The Koko Factor

Let's take a small break from the intense training you are being given to discuss more general realms of stupidity in the casinos from both the management side and the players' side. I will use Koko, a very famous gorilla, as the central character of what is coming up.

Koko is the lowland gorilla who supposedly has an IQ of between 85 and 95; this is based on an IQ test she took several years back. The average range for humans is 90 to 110. About 50 percent of the human population in America falls within that range, with about 25 percent above it and 25 percent below it. So Koko is, by our standards, a kind of dull normal individual, but she is, let's be frank, smarter than about 25 percent of the human population, which definitely includes the kid across the street from me, that strange neighbor of yours, and most of the kids you went to high school with.

I don't know if Koko is a smart gorilla or a stupid gorilla. For all I know, the average gorilla might have an IQ substantially higher than Koko's, but I do know this: if a human with Koko's IQ did the things Koko does, we'd call him—let's be frank now—stupid.

In my experience, I've seen some human Kokos in the casinos, and they aren't just on the players' side of the casino equation. There are some casino decision-makers who would be intellectually challenged by Koko. The overwhelming majority of casino workers I've met go from pretty smart to damn smart, but a few languish in the Koko ranges—the lowland intellectual gorilla fields.

These casino Kokos often do a great disservice to their players, their employees, and their industry, even though they have no awareness of this fact. They have instituted rules, regulations, and games that drive players away rather than bring players to them. In the interests of fairness, one must call a Koko a Koko if the name fits.

And I'm going to name names.

There is Bob...just kidding. I'm not naming names; even the Kokos have to eat. But what I will do now is name the policies that I think must have come from the Kokos of the casinos, as these decisions are, to be generous, cuckoo or Koko-nutty. Here goes:

Whoever first thought up the idea that in order to play two hands at blackjack you should have to play double the table minimum is a definite Koko. Really now, if the player wishes to play two hands, telling him he has to double his bet will often discourage him from doing so. The same player playing two hands makes just as much money for the casino as two players playing one hand each. It's the exact same thing! So why tell him he has to double his bet? It's stupid. Let him play two hands at the table minimum, and the casino makes twice as much money. Ask him to double his bet, and he might bet only one hand. Big players will play two hands at higher rates because they can afford to, so it won't discourage high-end two-hand play.

A truly Koko-esque moment occurred some years ago in Vegas when a casino proudly announced on a giant billboard that it was offering a single-deck blackjack game where a natural paid $6 to $5. Of course, a natural would usually pay $7.50 for $5, so this casino was trumpeting the fact that it was *screwing* the players big time. Just about then, many Strip casinos went to *continuous* automatic shufflers on their blackjack games to increase the number of hands a player played by 20 percent. And all the Strip casinos went to hitting Soft 17 to increase profits at blackjack as well. And in the years since these "profit-enhancing" rules went into effect, what has happened? Instead of an increase in blackjack profits, the Vegas casinos have lost blackjack revenue! That sound you hear are the Kokos who created these "improvements" slipping on banana peels!

Yes, there are Kokos in every industry and line of work. I'm sure many of you, when you meet with your extended families, can point out the Kokos in your clan. Still, a gorilla is a gorilla. They are fun to watch as they swing on a tree limb and pound their chests and uproot logs looking for succulent bugs. But do you really want them in positions of authority? Uhaheehgagump! (That's gorilla for "NO WAY!")

But there are as many casino-player Kokos too. They can teach us just how stupid we players can be. The real Koko was raised by humans and taught American Sign Language, so she can actually communicate. Her active vocabulary is about 500 words, and she never says things like what teenagers say, "Well, like, you know, like I said, like, I wasn't, like, going to do that, like why should I?" or "That's phat!"

For a gorilla, Koko seems pretty savvy.

However, in a position of authority, Koko just couldn't hack it because, although she may be smart in gorilla terms, she's no world-beater in human terms. You don't want someone with an 85 IQ flying planes, doing brain surgery, or making decisions in the casinos—especially a gorilla. I don't want to be comped a banana.

But to be fair to casino executives, there are plenty of Koko players in the casinos, and they are far more *visible* as they swing from machine to machine, game to game, causing havoc to their bankrolls and anyone who happens to make a decision at blackjack that is actually correct!

So this is dedicated to that breed of gorilla who makes gaming unpleasant not only for himself but for thee, me, and the dealers as well. I have heard every quote coming up with my own ears, and I have seen every event with my own eyes.

At blackjack, the Koko is convinced he knows what's best for the table and does not hesitate to give you advice. "Never hit a 16 against a dealer's 7," he scolds as you look at your hand of 16 and see the dealer's 7 staring you in the face. In his own game, he has such peculiar moves as splitting tens and not splitting aces or 8s against a dealer's 9, 10, or ace. And when you attempt to so split against said hands, he'll gently chide you with, "What're ya, stoop-pid?"

The Koko is convinced that the dealer has a 10-valued card under every up-card, even though the 10-valued cards make up a mere 31 percent of the shoe. If you make a move he doesn't like, and you happen to lose, God help you; he'll jump on it. "See, see, what'd I tell ya?" Should a 10-valued card actually be under the up-card, you won't hear the end of it: "The dealer *always* has a 10 in the hole!"

At craps the Koko continually presses his bets, before he ever takes down a win, because he's always looking for the monster roll, the hot hand that comes about once a month or so when random rollers shoot, and he always wants to make a killing, not just a profit. And when he loses his thrice-pressed bets to a seven-out, he moans and complains about all the rotten shooters. "Can't anyone shoot the dice?" Of course, when *he* shoots, it's a different story; he tries to pretend he doesn't care whether he wins or loses. He just flings the dice indifferently toward the other end of the table. It's almost as if he wishes to seven-out so he can go back to bitching and moaning about everyone else.

The Koko at roulette will cover every number, figuring he has to win on each and every spin. He doesn't realize that the house pays only 35 units on a win, but he loses 37 units at the same time.

The Koko at a slot machine is a marvel to behold as he yells and hits the machine. "This damn thing is cold, ice cold," he complains as he puts another $100 bill into the bill changer. If asked why he doesn't just abandon the machine and look for greener pastures elsewhere, he states confidently: "Because this machine is *due* to hit!"

The Koko has an annoying habit at the machines. If someone else is winning, he goes over to that person and hovers around them, hoping they will leave the machine and that he'll be able to take it over. "That's how I get on hot machines," he says confidentially, pulling out his ATM card to take yet another advance.

The Koko blames everyone and everything for his losses; everything, that is, but himself and his poor strategies. At blackjack, the third baseman caused him to lose because of the way he played his cards. At craps, the shooters stink. At roulette, the wheel is "off." At slots, the machines are jinxed!

The Koko's most irritating trait is the fact that he thinks everyone gives two flying cents about *his* luck! He thinks he is the center of the gambling universe. Everyone should applaud his good luck, while his bad luck should bring on the sympathy from everyone. Unlike Job from the Bible, the Koko-nut enjoys the attention even horrendous luck brings him because that places him where he wants to be—in *your* face.

When he asks for a comp that is outrageously above his betting levels and playing time, he rails when the pit boss offers him the buffet instead.

"I should get the steakhouse, at the very least!" he'll scream, when what he really deserves is "a trough of baked beans garnished with a couple of dead dogs." (I got that line from the great British comedy *Fawlty Towers*!)

The Koko makes casino gambling an unpleasant experience for the rest of us because his fate and face are always intruding into our space. He isn't just interested in what he's doing; he wants to make sure you are too.

The Koko knows everything there is to know about gambling, politics, religion, philosophy, medicine, computers, love, and relationships. He can read the future: "I knew that was gonna happen!" And he knows the past: "This *always* happens!"

So what is the typical human player to do when confronted with a Koko at the tables? Get up and swing over to someplace where he isn't.

So what is the difference between a ploppy and a Koko? Nothing really. Both are names to call people who annoy us.

Okay, your break is over. Back to the learning process.

CHAPTER 11

Optimum Basic Strategy (OBS)

Dan Pronovost has come up with a new Basic Strategy that can be played *only with Speed Count* that enhances your edge at the game and also gives you built-in camouflage to throw the pit off to the fact that you are a highly skilled player.

Although you can play traditional Basic Strategies with Speed Count, the Optimum Basic Strategy (OBS) is the best way to gain even more of an edge when you play Speed Count.

OBS is subtly different for different games. You don't have to memorize the changes from the traditional Basic Strategy to play perfectly—in fact, you don't have to memorize anything.

If you thought Basic Strategy was the Bible cast in stone, the mere suggestion of variations may seem like heresy. How can you make more money by playing differently when Basic Strategy has been established for years? It turns out that there is a big difference between optimizing your fixed playing strategy as a card counter and as a non-counter. OBS is exactly that—a fixed playing strategy that is somewhat different from the traditional Basic Strategy but one that will give you a greater edge when you use Speed Count. Again, OBS can *only* be used with Speed Count.

When most card counters learn their craft, they spend a lot of time memorizing changes in the Basic Strategy based on the count to enhance their edge. These are called "index plays," and they are notoriously difficult for many blackjack card counters to master. Playing these incorrectly brings errors in your play, and errors result in losses.

Dan Pronovost has made changing strategies in midstream unnecessary because the OBS is based on what the best play of each hand is all the time. You will note some unusual plays in the OBS, but because you are using Speed Count, these plays will make you more money than the traditional Basic Strategy. Using the OBS also makes you look like a regular player—and a somewhat dim one at that.

What follows is the Optimum Basic Strategy for all types of blackjack games. The changes from the traditional Basic Strategy will be marked with an asterisk.

Many pit bosses, floor people, dealers, and other players will ask to look at your OBS reference cards (if you use one), and they will notice that some of your plays are "wrong." That is good. Just act like a dope and insist that you intend to play these hands just the way the card says to.

Optimum Basic Strategy
S=Stand; H=hit; D=Double Down; P=Split; U=Surrender
Game is 2-4-6-8 decks; dealer HITS on Soft 17; double after splits allowed

For boxes with a slash, use play on the left if permitted; if not, use play on the right.

Hand	2	3	4	5	6	7	8	9	10	Ace
8	H	H	H	H	*D/H	H	H	H	H	H
9	*D/H	D/H	D/H	D/H	D/H	H	H	H	H	H
10	D/H	D/H	D/H	D/H	D/H	D/H	D/H	D/H	H	H
11	D/H	D/H	D/H	D/H	D/H	D/H	D/H	D/H	D/H	*D/H
12	H	*S	S	S	S	H	H	H	H	H
13	S	S	S	S	S	H	H	H	H	H
14	S	S	S	S	S	H	H	H	H	H
15	S	S	S	S	S	H	H	H	U/H	*U/H
16	S	S	S	S	S	H	H	U/H	*U/S	U/H
17	S	S	S	S	S	S	S	S	S	S
A-2	H	H	H	D/H	D/H	H	H	H	H	H
A-3	H	H	*D/H	D/H	D/H	H	H	H	H	H
A-4	H	H	D/H	D/H	D/H	H	H	H	H	H
A-5	H	H	D/H	D/H	D/H	H	H	H	H	H
A-6	H	D/H	D/H	D/H	D/H	H	H	H	H	H
A-7	*D/S	D/S	D/S	D/S	D/S	S	S	H	H	H
A-8	S	S	S	S	*D/S	S	S	S	S	S
A-9	S	S	S	S	S	S	S	S	S	S
A-A	P	P	P	P	P	P	P	P	P	P
2-2	P	P	P	P	P	P	H	H	H	H
3-3	P	P	P	P	P	P	H	H	H	H
4-4	H	H	H	P	P	H	H	H	H	H
5-5	D/H	D/H	D/H	D/H	D/H	D/H	D/H	D/H	H	H
6-6	P	P	P	P	P	H	H	H	H	H
7-7	P	P	P	P	P	P	*P	H	*U/H	*U/H
8-8	P	P	P	P	P	P	P	P	*U/P	*U/P
9-9	P	P	P	P	P	S	P	P	S	S
10-10	S	S	S	S	S	S	S	S	S	S

Optimum Basic Strategy
S=Stand; H=Hit; D=Double Down; P=Split; U=Surrender

Game is 2-4-6-8 decks; dealer HITS on Soft 17; no double after splits allowed

For boxes with a slash, use play on the left if permitted; if not, use play on the right.

Hand	2	3	4	5	6	7	8	9	10	Ace
8	H	H	H	H	*D/H	H	H	H	H	H
9	*D/H	D/H	D/H	D/H	D/H	H	H	H	H	H
10	D/H	D/H	D/H	D/H	D/H	D/H	D/H	D/H	H	H
11	D/H	D/H	D/H	D/H	D/H	D/H	D/H	D/H	D/H	*D/H
12	H	*S	S	S	S	H	H	H	H	H
13	S	S	S	S	S	H	H	H	H	H
14	S	S	S	S	S	H	H	H	H	H
15	S	S	S	S	S	H	H	H	U/H	*U/H
16	S	S	S	S	S	H	H	U/H	*U/S	U/H
17	S	S	S	S	S	S	S	S	S	S
A-2	H	H	H	D/H	D/H	H	H	H	H	H
A-3	H	H	*D/H	D/H	D/H	H	H	H	H	H
A-4	H	H	D/H	D/H	D/H	H	H	H	H	H
A-5	H	H	D/H	D/H	D/H	H	H	H	H	H
A-6	H	D/H	D/H	D/H	D/H	H	H	H	H	H
A-7	*D/S	D/S	D/S	D/S	D/S	S	S	H	H	H
A-8	S	S	S	S	*D/S	S	S	S	S	S
A-9	S	S	S	S	S	S	S	S	S	S
A-A	P	P	P	P	P	P	P	P	P	P
2-2	H	H	P	P	P	P	H	H	H	H
3-3	H	H	P	P	P	P	H	H	H	H
4-4	H	H	H	H	D/H	H	H	H	H	H
5-5	D/H	D/H	D/H	D/H	*D/H	D/H	D/H	D/H	H	H
6-6	P	P	P	P	P	H	H	H	H	H
7-7	P	P	P	P	P	P	H	H	*U/H	*U/H
8-8	P	P	P	P	P	P	P	P	*U/P	*UP
9-9	P	P	P	P	P	S	P	P	S	S
10-10	S	S	S	S	S	S	S	S	S	S

Optimum Basic Strategy
S=Stand; H=Hit; D=Double Down; P=Split; U=Surrender
Game is 2-4-6-8 decks; dealer STANDS on 17; double after splits allowed

For boxes with a slash, use play on the left if permitted; if not, use play on the right.

Hand	2	3	4	5	6	7	8	9	10	Ace
8	H	H	H	H	*D/H	H	H	H	H	H
9	*D/H	D/H	D/H	D/H	D/H	H	H	H	H	H
10	D/H	D/H	D/H	D/H	D/H	D/H	D/H	D/H	H	H
11	D/H	D/H	D/H	D/H	D/H	D/H	D/H	D/H	D/H	*D/H
12	H	*S	S	S	S	H	H	H	H	H
13	S	S	S	S	S	H	H	H	H	H
14	S	S	S	S	S	H	H	H	H	H
15	S	S	S	S	S	H	H	H	U/H	*U/H
16	S	S	S	S	S	H	H	U/H	*U/S	U/H
17	S	S	S	S	S	S	S	S	S	S
A-2	H	H	H	D/H	D/H	H	H	H	H	H
A-3	H	H	*D/H	D/H	D/H	H	H	H	H	H
A-4	H	H	D/H	D/H	D/H	H	H	H	H	H
A-5	H	H	D/H	D/H	D/H	H	H	H	H	H
A-6	H	D/H	D/H	D/H	D/H	H	H	H	H	H
A-7	*D/S	D/S	D/S	D/S	D/S	S	S	H	H	H
A-8	S	S	S	S	*D/S	S	S	S	S	S
A-9	S	S	S	S	S	S	S	S	S	S
A-A	P	P	P	P	P	P	P	P	P	P
2-2	P	P	P	P	P	P	H	H	H	H
3-3	P	P	P	P	P	P	H	H	H	H
4-4	H	H	H	P	P	H	H	H	H	H
5-5	D/H	D/H	D/H	D/H	D/H	D/H	D/H	D/H	H	H
6-6	P	P	P	P	P	H	H	H	H	H
7-7	P	P	P	P	P	P	H	H	*U/H	*U/H
8-8	P	P	P	P	P	P	P	P	*U/P	*U/P
9-9	P	P	P	P	P	S	P	P	S	S
10-10	S	S	S	S	S	S	S	S	S	S

Optimum Basic Strategy
S=Stand; H=Hit; D=Double Down; P=Split; U=Surrender

Game is 2-4-6-8 decks; dealer STANDS on Soft 17; no double after splits allowed

For boxes with a slash, use play on the left if permitted; if not, use play on the right.

Hand	2	3	4	5	6	7	8	9	10	Ace
8	H	H	H	H	*D/H	H	H	H	H	H
9	*D/H	D/H	D/H	D/H	D/H	H	H	H	H	H
10	D/H	D/H	D/H	D/H	D/H	D/H	D/H	D/H	H	H
11	D/H	D/H	D/H	D/H	D/H	D/H	D/H	D/H	D/H	*D/H
12	H	*S	S	S	S	H	H	H	H	H
13	S	S	S	S	S	H	H	H	H	H
14	S	S	S	S	S	H	H	H	H	H
15	S	S	S	S	S	H	H	H	U/H	*U/H
16	S	S	S	S	S	H	H	U/H	*U/S	U/H
17	S	S	S	S	S	S	S	S	S	S
A-2	H	H	H	D/H	D/H	H	H	H	H	H
A-3	H	H	*D/H	D/H	D/H	H	H	H	H	H
A-4	H	H	D/H	D/H	D/H	H	H	H	H	H
A-5	H	H	D/H	D/H	D/H	H	H	H	H	H
A-6	H	D/H	D/H	D/H	D/H	H	H	H	H	H
A-7	*D/S	D/S	D/S	D/S	D/S	S	S	H	H	H
A-8	S	S	S	S	*D/S	S	S	S	S	S
A-9	S	S	S	S	S	S	S	S	S	S
A-A	P	P	P	P	P	P	P	P	P	P
2-2	H	H	P	P	P	P	H	H	H	H
3-3	H	H	P	P	P	P	H	H	H	H
4-4	H	H	H	H	*D/H	H	H	H	H	H
5-5	D/H	D/H	D/H	D/H	D/H	D/H	D/H	D/H	H	H
6-6	*P	P	P	P	P	H	H	H	H	H
7-7	P	P	P	P	P	P	H	H	*U/H	*U/H
8-8	P	P	P	P	P	P	P	P	*U/P	P
9-9	P	P	P	P	P	S	P	P	S	S
10-10	S	S	S	S	S	S	S	S	S	S

Optimum Basic Strategy
S=Stand; H=Hit; D=Double Down; P=Split; U=Surrender
Game is SINGLE deck; dealer HITS on Soft 17; no double after splits allowed

For boxes with a slash, use play on the left if permitted; if not, use play on the right.

Hand	2	3	4	5	6	7	8	9	10	Ace
8	H	H	H	D/H	D/H	H	H	H	H	H
9	D/H	D/H	D/H	D/H	D/H	H	H	H	H	H
10	D/H	D/H	D/H	D/H	D/H	D/H	D/H	D/H	H	H
11	D/H	D/H	D/H	D/H	D/H	D/H	D/H	D/H	D/H	D/H
12	H	H	S	S	S	H	H	H	H	H
13	S	S	S	S	S	H	H	H	H	H
14	S	S	S	S	S	H	H	H	H	H
15	S	S	S	S	S	H	H	H	*U/H	*U/H
16	S	S	S	S	S	H	H	*U/H	U/H	*U/H
17	S	S	S	S	S	S	S	S	S	S
A-2	H	H	D/H	D/H	D/H	H	H	H	H	H
A-3	H	H	D/H	D/H	D/H	H	H	H	H	H
A-4	H	H	D/H	D/H	D/H	H	H	H	H	H
A-5	H	H	D/H	D/H	D/H	H	H	H	H	H
A-6	D/H	D/H	D/H	D/H	D/H	H	H	H	H	H
A-7	S	D/S	D/S	D/S	D/S	S	S	H	H	H
A-8	S	S	S	*D/S	D/S	S	S	S	S	S
A-9	S	S	S	S	S	S	S	S	S	S
A-A	P	P	P	P	P	P	P	P	P	P
2-2	H	P	P	P	P	P	H	H	H	H
3-3	H	H	P	P	P	P	H	H	H	H
4-4	H	H	H	D/H	D/H	H	H	H	H	H
5-5	D/H	D/H	D/H	D/H	D/H	D/H	D/H	D/H	H	H
6-6	P	P	P	P	P	H	H	H	H	H
7-7	P	P	P	P	P	P	H	H	U/S	*U/H
8-8	P	P	P	P	P	P	P	P	P	P
9-9	P	P	P	P	P	S	P	P	S	*P
10-10	S	S	S	S	S	S	S	S	S	S

Optimum Basic Strategy
S=Stand; H=Hit; D=Double Down; P=Split; U=Surrender

Game is SINGLE deck; dealer HITS on Soft 17; double after splits allowed

For boxes with a slash, use play on the left if permitted; if not, use play on the right.

Hand	2	3	4	5	6	7	8	9	10	Ace
8	H	H	H	D/H	D/H	H	H	H	H	H
9	D/H	D/H	D/H	D/H	D/H	H	H	H	H	H
10	D/H	D/H	D/H	D/H	D/H	D/H	D/H	D/H	H	H
11	D/H	D/H	D/H	D/H	D/H	D/H	D/H	D/H	D/H	D/H
12	H	H	S	S	S	H	H	H	H	H
13	S	S	S	S	S	H	H	H	H	H
14	S	S	S	S	S	H	H	H	H	H
15	S	S	S	S	S	H	H	H	*U/H	*U/H
16	S	S	S	S	S	H	H	*U/H	U/H	*U/H
17	S	S	S	S	S	S	S	S	S	S
A-2	H	H	D/H	D/H	D/H	H	H	H	H	H
A-3	H	H	D/H	D/H	D/H	H	H	H	H	H
A-4	H	H	D/H	D/H	D/H	H	H	H	H	H
A-5	H	H	D/H	D/H	D/H	H	H	H	H	H
A-6	D/H	D/H	D/H	D/H	D/H	H	H	H	H	H
A-7	S	D/S	D/S	D/S	D/S	S	S	H	H	H
A-8	S	S	S	*D/S	D/S	S	S	S	S	S
A-9	S	S	S	S	S	S	S	S	S	S
A-A	P	P	P	P	P	P	P	P	P	P
2-2	P	P	P	P	P	P	H	H	H	H
3-3	P	P	P	P	P	P	H	H	H	H
4-4	H	H	P	P	P	H	H	H	H	H
5-5	D/H	D/H	D/H	D/H	D/H	D/H	D/H	D/H	H	H
6-6	P	P	P	P	P	P	H	H	H	H
7-7	P	P	P	P	P	P	P	H	U/S	*U/H
8-8	P	P	P	P	P	P	P	P	P	P
9-9	P	P	P	P	P	S	P	P	S	*P
10-10	S	S	S	S	S	S	S	S	S	S

Optimum Basic Strategy
S=Stand; H=Hit; D=Double Down; P=Split; U=Surrender
Game is SINGLE deck; dealer STANDS on 17; double after splits allowed

For boxes with a slash, use play on the left if permitted; if not, use play on the right.

Hand	2	3	4	5	6	7	8	9	10	Ace
8	H	H	H	D/H	D/H	H	H	H	H	H
9	D/H	D/H	D/H	D/H	D/H	H	H	H	H	H
10	D/H	D/H	D/H	D/H	D/H	D/H	D/H	D/H	H	H
11	D/H	D/H	D/H	D/H	D/H	D/H	D/H	D/H	D/H	D/H
12	H	H	S	S	S	H	H	H	H	H
13	S	S	S	S	S	H	H	H	H	H
14	S	S	S	S	S	H	H	H	H	H
15	S	S	S	S	S	H	H	H	*U/H	*U/H
16	S	S	S	S	S	H	H	*U/H	U/H	*U/H
17	S	S	S	S	S	S	S	S	S	S
A-2	H	H	D/H	D/H	D/H	H	H	H	H	H
A-3	H	H	D/H	D/H	D/H	H	H	H	H	H
A-4	H	H	D/H	D/H	D/H	H	H	H	H	H
A-5	H	H	D/H	D/H	D/H	H	H	H	H	H
A-6	D/H	D/H	D/H	D/H	D/H	H	H	H	H	H
A-7	S	D/S	D/S	D/S	D/S	S	S	H	H	H
A-8	S	S	S	*D/S	D/S	S	S	S	S	S
A-9	S	S	S	S	S	S	S	S	S	S
A-A	P	P	P	P	P	P	P	P	P	P
2-2	P	P	P	P	P	P	H	H	H	H
3-3	P	P	P	P	P	P	H	H	H	H
4-4	H	H	P	P	P	H	H	H	H	H
5-5	D/H	D/H	D/H	D/H	D/H	D/H	D/H	D/H	H	H
6-6	P	P	P	P	P	P	H	H	H	H
7-7	P	P	P	P	P	P	P	H	U/S	*U/H
8-8	P	P	P	P	P	P	P	P	P	P
9-9	P	P	P	P	P	S	P	P	S	S
10-10	S	S	S	S	S	S	S	S	S	S

Optimum Basic Strategy
S=Stand; H=Hit; D=Double Down; P=Split; U=Surrender

Game is SINGLE deck; dealer STANDS on 17; no double after splits allowed

For boxes with a slash, use play on the left if permitted; if not, use play on the right.

Hand	2	3	4	5	6	7	8	9	10	Ace
8	H	H	H	D/H	D/H	H	H	H	H	H
9	D/H	D/H	D/H	D/H	D/H	H	H	H	H	H
10	D/H	D/H	D/H	D/H	D/H	D/H	D/H	D/H	H	H
11	D/H	D/H	D/H	D/H	D/H	D/H	D/H	D/H	D/H	D/H
12	H	H	S	S	S	H	H	H	H	H
13	S	S	S	S	S	H	H	H	H	H
14	S	S	S	S	S	H	H	H	H	H
15	S	S	S	S	S	H	H	H	*U/H	*U/H
16	S	S	S	S	S	H	H	*U/H	U/H	*U/H
17	S	S	S	S	S	S	S	S	S	S
A-2	H	H	D/H	D/H	D/H	H	H	H	H	H
A-3	H	H	D/H	D/H	D/H	H	H	H	H	H
A-4	H	H	D/H	D/H	D/H	H	H	H	H	H
A-5	H	H	D/H	D/H	D/H	H	H	H	H	H
A-6	D/H	D/H	D/H	D/H	D/H	H	H	H	H	H
A-7	S	D/S	D/S	D/S	D/S	S	S	H	H	H
A-8	S	S	S	*D/S	D/S	S	S	S	S	S
A-9	S	S	S	S	S	S	S	S	S	S
A-A	P	P	P	P	P	P	P	P	P	P
2-2	H	P	P	P	P	P	H	H	H	H
3-3	H	H	P	P	P	P	H	H	H	H
4-4	H	H	H	D/P	D/P	H	H	H	H	H
5-5	D/H	D/H	D/H	D/H	D/H	D/H	D/H	D/H	H	H
6-6	P	P	P	P	P	H	H	H	H	H
7-7	P	P	P	P	P	P	H	H	U/S	*U/H
8-8	P	P	P	P	P	P	P	P	P	P
9-9	P	P	P	P	P	S	P	P	S	S
10-10	S	S	S	S	S	S	S	S	S	S

CHAPTER 12

Bankroll Requirements and Risk of Ruin (ROR)

I mentioned this before, but it is good to mention it again. You can lose. You can have a losing session today. You can have several losing sessions in a row—today, tonight, and all day tomorrow. You can have a losing trip. You can have many losing trips—even in a row. The fact that you have an edge does not guarantee that each and every time you step up to the blackjack table that you are going to win. Having an edge means that in the long run you will come out ahead. In the short run, your head can be handed to you.

What prevents astute advantage players from going nuts when they hit those inevitable losing streaks is the fact that they have an adequate bankroll to sustain them while Lady Luck flogs them unmercifully. They also have what I call a strong *emotional bankroll* that allows them to take the losses in stride. You must have both a real and *sufficient* monetary bankroll and also an emotional bankroll to survive the fluctuations that you will experience when you play advantage blackjack.

If you are underfinanced, you can have your bankroll wiped out. That's right, even with an edge a bad streak can come along that wipes you out. You must have plenty of money behind you to be able to withstand the losing streaks.

Let me give you a simple but powerful example of what I am talking about. Let us say you want to engage your nephew, the highly annoying

Little Timmy, in a game of flip-the-coin. Each flip is for $1. If you win, you win $1. However, we want to give Little Timmy a giant edge over you, so every time he wins, he receives $1.10. Wow! Your bankroll for this contest is $1,000,000,000. His bankroll is $2. He has a very large mathematical edge over you. He is also doomed to lose. The first sustained losing streak is going to put annoying Little Timmy away. He just doesn't have the bankroll to engage in the contest with you. He could lose the first two tosses, and he'd be a dead man, er, kid.

The same is true of any advantage player at blackjack. You have to have the edge *plus* a sufficient bankroll to win. That's the bottom line of winning play.

The mathematicians call having a sufficient bankroll a part of their Risk of Ruin (ROR) formula. Risk of Ruin is just that. Given X amount of money and betting this particular spread at the game, what are the chances that I will wind up like the annoying Little Timmy—dead broke and crying my eyes out? If I want to bet $10 to $40 using Speed Count in a double-deck game, how much will I need in my bankroll for 100 hands, for 200 hands, for 2,000 hands, for 20,000 hands, and for 2 million hands to assure me that I can last at the game no matter how fickle Lady Luck gets?

I have to tell you a little story about my blackjack-playing career to give you a sense of how awful losing one's entire gambling stake can be. The mathematicians say "Risk of Ruin," and that is a clean way of really saying, "I got my ass kicked hard!" Here's my story:

When my wife, the beautiful A.P. and I gave up theater for the joys of challenging the casinos using advantage play, we put aside $5,000 as our bankroll. This was in the 1980s. We worked on our Hi-Lo card counting, and I memorized 4 zillion strategy changes from Basic Strategy based on the count (these changes are called "indices" by the blackjack cognoscenti). We then went to Atlantic City, the Queen of Resorts.

In those glorious days of the 1980s, Atlantic City was not a 24/7 town. It was a 20/7 or an 18/7 town or something like that. It also had some wonderful deeply penetrated four-deck games with surrender, great rules, and non-paranoid pit bosses if you were betting red and small green action, which we were. My bet spread was 1-to-8 on the four-deck games, $10 to $80, enough to give me an edge.

We stayed in Atlantic City for nine days and destroyed them. I don't think we lost a session. We'd play about eight or nine hours a day, and I really thought to myself, *I am going to become a billionaire! This card counting is so easy and profitable. You know, I might even buy myself a casino.*

When we came home, I decided to schedule another trip right away. This time we went for 16 days. The *worst* 16 days of my blackjack-playing life! We lost and lost and lost. I started to bet bigger than I had planned in high counts, which heavily favored me—and lost. I would wait for the casinos to open in the morning and be the first at the tables. And lost. I played all day long. I played most of the night.

And lost.

I lost all the money we had won on our last trip and all the money we had saved to be professional gamblers. Although I was not broke in my real life, I had lost all the money I had set aside for my gambling life. On the way back home, we stopped off at the Captain's house (he was my gambling mentor) where he gave A.P. and me a lesson about gambling and human rhythm that we have never forgotten. He also taught us about bankroll requirements.

I was underfinanced in those days—or I was betting too big for the money I did have. I was also out of my mind because I thought, *Things have to change! Things have to get better! I will bet more and get all my money back!* Yes, I was dumb. Despite having an edge over the house, I lost my very first gambling bankroll—every single penny of it.

You'll note that while I was a partner with the beautiful A.P., I can't put any of the blame for the loss on her. She wanted to play conservatively. She wanted our bets to be based on sound principles. She wanted to play relaxed, normal-length sessions. I was the one who had lost his cool and our cash.

Today, I have another bankroll, one that I will never be able to lose in the casinos because I no longer play like a fool and bet like a madman in relation to that bankroll. I discovered in those heady days of the 1980s that losing my money emotionally hurts me more than winning money makes me happy. The negative is stronger than the positive for me. Knowing this, I have given myself a strict rule—I have a zero Risk of Ruin for my bankroll. Zero. Zip. Aught. Cipher. Duck egg. Goose egg. Nada. Nadir. Naught. Nil. Nought. Zilch. Zot.

Please Note: *There really is no zero Risk of Ruin, but you can get it down to thousandths of a percentage, which is the same thing...almost.*

Zero risk makes me feel good. It allows me to play perfectly.

Many card counters, when they hear me say this, think, *Scoblete is an idiot! He's betting too small for his bankroll if he has a zero Risk of Ruin.* Maybe so. But I never have to worry that I will be wiped out no matter how bad the current bad streak becomes. I need that kind of bankroll to allow me to have the *emotional bankroll* to play these casino games fearlessly—otherwise they aren't worth playing. I hate to lose money.

Let us say that you are playing a double-deck game, S17, DAS, and you want to play for four hours in a given day. You are a $10 bettor, and you will spread one to four units. To give you a 5 percent Risk of Ruin—which means a 5 percent chance of losing every penny in your session stake—you must have $1,064 for that day of play. If you have less, your chances of losing it all increase. If you were to give yourself an $890 bankroll for the day, your chance of losing it all zooms up to 10 percent. Yes, that means 10 percent of the time with a day's bankroll of $890 you will lose it all.

To make sure that you have enough money behind you, you need to look at three types of bankrolls:
1. Session bankroll
2. Trip bankroll
3. Total bankroll

Obviously, the most important bankroll is No. 3. How much money have you put aside for your advantage play at blackjack? Your total bankroll dictates what your betting level will be given the Risk of Ruin that you can tolerate. The trip bankroll is how much of your bankroll you will bring with you on your trips to the casinos, and your session bankroll is how much bankroll you will give yourself to play a given session or day.

If you were playing the two-deck game above, your lifetime Risk of Ruin at 5 percent would necessitate a total bankroll of approximately

$10,225. Personally, a 5 percent Risk of Ruin is way too much for me. Having once lost my entire bankroll, I want *fractions* of a percent!

Of course, you will win more money than you lose over time—I may not have stressed that much in this chapter—and your bankroll will go up. If you are comfortable with a 5 percent Risk of Ruin, you can increase your betting levels based on your total bankroll. Or, you can first reduce the percent of your risk by allowing your bankroll to grow without increasing your bet size. When you get to a 1 percent or half-percent or quarter-percent Risk of Ruin, you can then increase your bets accordingly. *You* have to decide how you want to proceed. Some of what you decide will not be based on math but on your emotional ability to bet certain amounts knowing that you can lose.

How do you know you are betting too much money? When you lose you think of other things you could have done with the money. *Gee*, you think, *I could have had that heart surgery I need.* If that happens, then you must reduce what you are wagering. Otherwise you might just have that heart attack due to the stress of wagering.

The 401G

If you want to be a serious advantage player, my recommendation to you is to start a 401G (the G stands for *gambling*). A 401G is a money-market checking account that you use for your gambling dollars. You should never be using "real" money when you play in the casinos; you should be using only money that you have set aside specifically for playing. This 401G can go a long way toward strengthening your emotional bankroll too. Knowing you have the proper amount of money in a single account to play at the level you feel comfortable will make you feel even more comfortable.

As you win money, you put it in your 401G; when you lose money, you lose it from your 401G. Now what should you do if you lose, say, 20 percent of your total bankroll in a horrendous series of defeats? A smart move would be to reduce your total betting by 20 percent so that your Risk of Ruin stays at 5 percent or whatever level you feel comfortable with. If you win and increase your 401G by 20 percent, you can increase your betting by this percentage as well.

CHAPTER 13

The Casinos Hate
Card Counters

Speed Count will give you the edge at the game of blackjack. You will win money in the long run. And the more you play, the better it is for you. I like that. I am sure you like that fact too. Speed Count is easy to learn and easy to use. It is a wonderful thing to be able to get the edge over the casino Goliath, isn't it? You are a little David, and the casinos are these big monsters—and you can beat them with your little Speed Count slingshot.

Of course, the casinos will hate you if they learn you can beat them. You understand that, right? Advantage players are the scum of the earth to the casino bosses. One boss recently called them "earners" with total disdain in his voice. Yes, they "earn" money because they can beat the casino games. In fact, they are smart. The casinos hate smart. Smart is bad.

Here is the casino thinking in other terms: "Lebron James should be banned from basketball because he is too good to play. We want losers on our team!"

The stories of card counters being back-roomed, beaten, harassed, and thrown out of their hotel rooms in the middle of the night are not fictions invented by the propeller hats. In the past (mostly), awful things were done to law-abiding citizens by the casino executives and security forces obsessed with protecting their games from advantage players who were not doing anything illegal.

The same smiling casino executive photographed with that smiling slot patron who has just won a million dollars on a machine will be the same guy snarling, foaming, sputtering, and spewing to a card counter whose expectation is $20 bucks an hour, "We don't want you here; you are too good for us." This same executive will tell bigger players, "I am reading you the trespass act, and if you show up here again we will arrest you for trespassing."

Yes, it's like being in high school again. The smart kids are hated; the dumb ones rule. Smart is bad. Dumb is good. The casinos are ploppy heaven.

Card counters and other advantage players are the bane of the casinos' existence. Yes, the casinos offer games for the public to play, but when some members of the public figure out how to beat those games, well, "Get your fat or skinny butt out of our casino!" scream the executives.

The casinos want losers. The casinos cater to losers. The casinos love losers.

The casinos hate winners. They hate earners. They hate smart.

If you learn Speed Count, you will be a winner. You will be an earner because you are smart.

Oh, yes, the casinos will boot policemen, firemen, teachers, doctors, nurses, military veterans, and Medal of Honor winners from their properties if these individuals can beat the games. Mother Theresa? Out! The casinos will boot those who have fought in our recent wars and those who ran into the World Trade Center to save the lives of their fellow citizens from the monstrous terrorism perpetrated there. It doesn't matter who these winning citizens are, the response is the same: "Out! Out! Out! You are too good for our games!" The casino executives don't care that their fellow citizens are being singled out for using their brains to beat the casinos' games. Their response is "OUT!"

It's a disgrace.

It's un-American.

It's nauseating.

It's immoral.

It's also the truth.

You could be Jesus Christ or Moses or Buddha, but if you can count cards, you won't be welcomed in the casinos. Go walk on water elsewhere!

Go part the sea elsewhere! Do your eightfold path in someone else's garden! *Out! Out! Out!*

Unfortunately, the law is on the casinos' side for the most part. These casino businesses are not public enterprises—they are private entities and, as such, they have the right to refuse service to anyone they want to. They can't discriminate because of your race, that's true, or your gender or religion or your handicapping condition. But they can discriminate against your brain and your skill.

The casino executives have several ways of handling a threat to their profits.

They can "ask" you not to play blackjack, yes, but they also might say, "You can play any other game here," or, if they want, they can *tell* you to get lost and not come back to their property ever again. Casinos cannot, however, drag you into the back room and pummel the living daylights out of you (yes, in the past this has happened to some unfortunate card counters) and, in fact, if a casino executive stops you from playing and then "requests" that you come to the back room, you have the right to ask if he is calling the police. If he is, tell him you'll wait right where you are until the police arrive.

Because card counting is not illegal, you cannot be arrested for such intelligent use of your brain. If a casino executive tells you to beat it, then just beat it. Don't argue with the executive—he isn't interested in your opinions. Don't even talk to the executive. And don't show him your Medal of Honor or plaque for saving the lives of your fellow Americans in the World Trade Center attack. It won't change his mind. Just take your chips and leave. You can come back tomorrow and cash your chips in. Or you can send a friend to cash in your chips. Leave.

Always be courteous. Never touch a casino employee in these situations, as the casino might press assault charges against you. Those grandly, massively, rock-solidly, muscled security people are very delicate at these times, and the casino might accuse you of attacking them. Use your brain and just get out of the casino.

Let me share with you some of the experiences the beautiful A.P. and I have had in the "we-hate-card-counters" world of the casinos.

The Beautiful A.P. and Me Team

From the middle 1980s through 2000, the beautiful A.P. and I were a great card-counting team. We'd spend more than 130 days per year in the casinos. We had an elaborate system of signals—verbal and physical. For example, if A.P. talked about the president and his wife doing something (or any couple or pair doing or saying something), the count was a +2; if she told me I was drinking too much or I need some water so I wouldn't become dehydrated, the count was a +7; if she touched my forearm, the count was a +4. There were layers upon layers of signals. A.P. would count, signal me, and I played the hands and did the betting. As all this was going on, I was talking to the dealer, the floor person, the pit boss. I barely looked at the cards.

That was our usual method of playing, although we sometimes changed things depending on the game we were playing.

In the early 1990s we were playing in a downtown Las Vegas casino that prided itself on taking any kind of action any kind of player wished to play. We were decent bettors, going from $25 on one hand to two hands of $300 when the count called for it. We were typical card counters, of course, using the Hi-Lo card-counting system.

We were playing a single-deck game. I had two bets of $300 each on the layout. Suddenly the dealer started throwing the cards into my face. I jerked backward and felt metal in my back. It was a gun held by a monstrously large, steroidally enhanced security guard. I turned to the beautiful A.P., who was as wide-eyed as I was. "Let's just walk right out the front door. Take the chips. The guy isn't going to shoot us with all those people around...I hope."

So we scooped up our chips and headed for the door, ignoring the dealer who seemed to be sneering and the security guard who was foaming and growling. Thankfully, we weren't shot. The next day we came back on another shift and cashed in our chips. We also sent in some of our friends to cash in some of our chips as well. We obviously never played in that casino again.

Two weeks later, this same casino's security guards roughed up two other card counters—sending them both to the hospital, one in serious condition. These card counters sued the casino, and the suit was settled out of court.

On the Strip, also in the early 1990s, I was playing at a sleazy, berserk-child-infested casino that was offering an excellent single-deck blackjack game. I had heard that the place was going to change the game in a few days to a six-deck game of a much poorer quality. I never played this place, but I figured why not take my shot at its good game before it disappeared. The beautiful A.P., who had standards, said, "I'm sorry, but there are a lot of great games in Vegas. I am not playing in that dump."

So I went it alone.

I started playing two hands at $5 each. With the first positive increase in the count, I went up in huge leaps. So when the true count was +1 (or any initial plus count), I went to $50 on both hands. When it was +2, I went to $100 on both hands; when it was +3, I went to $200. I maxed out at two hands of $300. I figured I'd burn out my welcome quickly, as this place was known for its paranoid pit people and executives. Counters and winning non-counters were shown the door so often the door started to look like a revolving door.

As fate would have it, those increases in my bets won right away. I went on a torrid winning streak. I got to play three games before I saw a parade of suits heading for the table. I knew I was about to be booted, so I threw a tip to the dealer, scooped up all my chips and headed for the cage (cashier).

One suit followed me right to the cage and stood behind me. As I cashed in my chips, I could see him counting them. He glared at me and was about to speak. I turned with my extremely thick wad of $100 bills and headed out the door.

Next door to this casino were a couple of dumpy little casinos. I went in the side door of the one closest, and damn if this suit wasn't following me. He had an intense look on his beady-eyed face. I left this little casino out the front door and started going south on the Strip. He continued to follow me.

In the early 1990s, I was not slightly overweight as I am now (okay, okay, I am now more than slightly overweight), and I was still hitting the heavy bag, although my boxing career had long ended. I ran five- to 10-mile races. I was in great shape. I knew I could beat this creep up. And now I was a little annoyed, bordering on anger, so I turned and walked right at him. I looked him in his weasel-eyes and said, "What are you going to do?" He spun around and headed back to his casino. Of course, had this happened this week I would have to say, "Go away or I will belly-whomp you!"

He was probably tailing me to get the license plate of my car and maybe find out my name. Anyway, that is what I am guessing.

I have to say that some of my actual bannings—where the casino tells me that should I return to that casino I will be arrested for trespass-ing—have been largely due to my own stupidity and greed. In Mississippi my partner Dominator and I got really, really (REALLY) greedy. From its opening in the 1990s, the beautiful A.P. and I hammered the venue. Several casinos were becoming our personal bank accounts. Then Dominator joined me in the early 2000s. With dice control and card counting, we did what players should never do—we took the casinos' money. (The beautiful A.P. left the casino wars the day my younger son graduated college. "I hate the casinos," she said. "I am now officially retired.")

Well, that all ended in a single week when we were banned from every casino in that Southern state. Indeed, at some casinos, muscular security guards escorted us out. At one casino, Henry Tamburin saved us from some really big brutes by driving us off the property as if he were driving in the Indianapolis 500. At another, about a dozen suits descended on us at a craps table and told us, "Go away, you bums!" Actually that is not exactly what they said. The lead executive was pretty nice. "Frank," he said, "I am a big fan of yours, but you have just been winning too much. You can't play here anymore."

I have the whole tale about my Mississippi gaming and gawking expe-riences during the great ice storm in my book *The Virgin Kiss*.

Yes, casinos hate winning players—meaning winning players who actually have a real edge over them. I have other tales, but I have been playing since the mid-1980s. That's a long stretch of almost constant play; I'm bound to have horrifying tales. In truth, I played 99.9 percent of the time without any hassles, especially since I rarely got greedy (Mississippi and the berserk-child–infested casino being two exceptions).

The Best Blackjack Game We Ever Played

Okay, I told you a few rotten tales of my card-counting days with a tra-ditional count. This is the beautiful A.P.'s and my experience with the greatest game ever.

In the 1990s, when the kids were going to private high schools and then on to college, we used to make "tuition runs." That was pressure.

The greatest summer we ever spent was eight weeks in 1991 (or thereabouts) at the old Maxim, where they dealt a single-deck game all the way to the bottom, and if they ran out of cards they just reshuffled the deck and kept dealing. The only card you didn't see was the burn card. I learned a little-known technique called "end play" at this game.

I got to play with some of the great card counters of those days, the greatest of which was the late Paul Keen, a man every blackjack authority went to in order to check statistics and facts. He was the only card counter I ever met who could actually follow cards through a shuffle in a six-deck game. (You never heard of him? Savor this: The great card-counting guru Ken Uston used to go to Paul Keen for advice!)

In that Maxim game you could spread your bets from $5 to $500 in one giant leap if you wished, and no casino suit cared that you were counting or leaping your bets like Superman leapt off tall buildings in a single bound. During that summer we averaged more than eight hours of play per day, each of us playing two hands. It was an amazing game with these rules:

- Dealer stood on Soft 17,
- Blackjack paid 3-to-2,
- Double on any first two cards,
- Double after splits,
- Resplit twice,
- Surrender on any first two cards,
- Free $1 coupon good at any store or restaurant at Maxim with every blackjack of $5 and over.

And, by heaven, a full range of other comps to boot.

We started that summer as red-chip players; we ended it as black-chip and purple-chip players making $300 to $500 bets with impunity and fearlessness. The beautiful A.P. had to sew our winnings in my suit from toe to collar because I was afraid to carry so much cash in a suitcase. (You've seen those movies where the giant suitcase is filled with $100 stacks after the great bank robbery.)

I've never run into a game like that since. I mean, even Basic Strategy players had an edge at the game. A Basic Strategy player could start at $500 per hand if he wanted to!

Four weeks after we left Vegas, the Maxim shut down that game. One's first thought would be that the card counters went nuts and took all the money—but that is far from the truth. Here's what actually happened in those eight weeks we spent in the Maxim heaven:

1. Only four single-deck tables were open. These were not always populated by card counters. There was a multitude of ploppies taking up those seats too.
2. There were four double-deck games with normal penetration and traditional Vegas rules but no surrender. These were always packed with the usual gang of suspects.
3. There were about eight six-deck games as well with no surrender and normal Vegas rules. These were always packed too.
4. The craps games (I recall three tables) were packed with players. Some heavy action here with players making all the high-house-edge Crazy Crapper bets. In fact, when professional wrestling came to town, those big guys would come to the Maxim and body-slam their bankrolls into the casino's treasury.
5. The slot aisles were filled with the wives, husbands, and friends of the table-game players.
6. There was even a small poker "room" with a table that was always filled to capacity.

In short, the Maxim was hopping! Money was flowing in torrents at all these table games and in all those slot machines. It was hard to get a hotel room—even in the deadly heat of a Las Vegas summer. Those single-deck games lured the players in—even the worst players came because they figured they had a chance to win at such a great game; even if they had no idea how to play any blackjack game. And when they couldn't get a seat at the single-deck game, did those players leave? Hell no; they went to the other tables to play.

The Maxim was the place to be that summer.

Then it ended. The Maxim went back to the normal Vegas games, the crowds departed, and the Maxim went bankrupt in a couple of years, closed its doors, and was then sold to the Westin chain.

But for that summer, it was the only and the greatest game in town!

Do *You* Need to Worry?

Now, will *you* have to really worry about being asked not to play? Will you be banned or carted out by burly beastly steroidal security guards? Highly unlikely—very highly unlikely.

Henry, Dominator, Dan, and I have been playing Speed Count for years now, and we have experienced no problems with it. If you use your head and don't give any casino sustained action hour after hour, it will be very hard for the pit to see that you are playing with an edge when you use this method. Yes, it is possible that you might get nailed (the more aggressively you bet, the better your chances of this happening), and, if so, welcome to the club, as all good card counters have occasionally been "asked" to stop playing.

The best recommendation we can make is to keep your sessions at no more than 45 minutes to an hour long. If you are a high-roller, a half-hour session *and out* is a good way to go. It does take the casino some time to analyze your play and see that you have the edge over the game. If you are a rated player at the black-chip level, you should spread out your play on different shifts. Give the casino a moving target.

When you are playing the Speed Count and the OBS, remember that you are doing many things no card counters do. You have built-in camouflage protecting you because of these things:
1. You are sitting at first base (if possible).
2. You are not watching the cards as they are dealt.
3. You aren't interested in the sums of the hands of the other players or of the dealer.
4. Your first increased bets at 31 are at a count the casino software will probably not be aware of.

You also have a monstrous camouflage element in the Optimum Basic Strategy that we have given you. The OBS is something that not only increases your edge with Speed Count but also makes you look like a *poor* Basic Strategy player; in short, you look something like all the rest of the ploppies. Standing on 16 versus a dealer's 10-card, doubling on your 8s, and doubling your A:8 at times will make you look pretty stupid to the floor person or pit boss.

Memorize this: In the casinos, "stupid" is a synonym for "good." Be proud to appear stupid.

The Optimum Basic Strategy is a key element in camouflage. It's a wonderful thing—OBS increases your edge and makes you look dopey.

12 Other Camouflage Techniques

Those of you who have read other blackjack books know that traditional card counters spend a lot of time figuring out ways to fool the pit into thinking they aren't card counters. The great advantage player John May, author of *Get the Edge at Blackjack*, summed it all up by saying, "You play blackjack against the dealer and poker against the pit boss."

As a Speed-Counting blackjack player betting conservatively (or close to conservatively), we don't think you need to worry about camouflage because there is great built-in camouflage with Speed Count and the OBS. Using other camouflage techniques might just make your small edge even smaller.

Aggressive players betting green, black, and purple (plus) levels might want to follow some principles that gamblers use. You can mix and match these. Conservative bettors can use some of these as well—the ones that don't cost you money. (I have starred* the ones that cost you money.)

1.* When the count goes up, increase your bet if you won the last hand. If you lost the last hand, do not increase your bet.

2.* If count goes up and you lost, add only a half unit.

3.* If the count is high and you have a big bet up and the cut card comes out, do not lower your bet for the start of a new shoe.

4. Distribute your bets unevenly on two hands. Rarely do counters play two hands of unequal wagers.

5. Always be friendly to the pit. Casinos think that card counters tend to be somewhat standoffish.

6. You can talk about good or bad luck—but never mention skill.

7. Use an OBS card. Explain that you made it up to help you. When the pit boss looks at the OBS card he will see "mistakes." Good!

8. If you have hammered the casino in a high count and you have a nice profit, consider leaving and heading for another casino. A big win brings attention.

9.* If you push a hand with a big bet out and the count goes down, do not lower your bet. Gamblers usually keep the same units up.

10.* If you push a hand and the count goes up, leave the same bet up. Gamblers rarely increase bets after pushes.

11.* Do not do play deviations from OBS to make you look stupid. You look stupid enough when using the OBS. Play variations cost you too much money.

12. Feel free to bitch and moan when you lose hands. That's normal behavior in the casinos.

12 Things You Must Avoid at the Blackjack Tables

There are some things you should never say.

1. "What's the count?"
2. "Stop dealing so fast; I can't keep the count."
3. "Do you give good penetration?"
4. "...29, 30, 31, 33, 37—Hooray! Time to bet big!"
5. "Am I moving my lips as I add up the cards?"
6. "I count cards, so when I raise my bets, all of you at the table should raise your bets too."
7. "Hey, stop spreading hands; it makes it hard to keep my count."
8. "I only take insurance in high counts."
9. "You won't throw me out because I'm counting cards, will you?"
10. "Hey everyone, Speed Count is so easy to use to get an edge at blackjack!"
11. "My real name is Ken Uston, and I'm ready to play!"
12. "I am good friends with Frank Scoblete, Henry Tamburin, Dan Pronovost, and Dominator! Deal the cards, baby!"

CHAPTER 14

Blackjack Superstitions

lackjack superstitions are good to *pretend* to believe in when you are at the tables. It just makes you appear stupid, a thing we harp on. Stupid is good. Smart is bad. These superstitions are stupid. That is good—as long as you don't really believe them, which would be bad. I think that made sense; didn't it?

The Superstition: *Bad players at the table will cause you to lose.*
The Truth: The third baseman has a 16 and the dealer is showing a 6 as his up-card. The third baseman decides to hit and gets a 10, busting him. The dealer turns over his hole card and has a 10. The dealer now has 16. The dealer takes a hit and gets a 5, making his hand a 21.

Is the third baseman, who is obviously a poor player, responsible for your losing?

If you said yes, you are wrong.

Take a look at the scenario. There are two cards that can come up next, a 5 or a 10, or a 10 and a 5. We don't know what order the cards are in. If the third baseman decides to hit, there is a 50-50 chance he will get the 5 and the dealer will get the 10, or there is a 50-50 chance that the third baseman will get the 10 and the dealer will get the 5.

If the third baseman decides to stand, there is a 50-50 chance that the dealer will get the 5 and a 50-50 chance that the dealer will get the 10, busting him.

It's 50-50 no matter what the third baseman does.

The Superstition: *A new player entering a game in the middle of the shoe screws up the order of the cards.*

The Truth: Okay, go back to the example above. There are two cards that might come out, a 5 or a 10. Instead of the third baseman making a poor move, a new player entered the game just before this round was dealt. What card will the dealer get? If the new player can screw up the order of the cards, should those two cards be changed in some way? But they aren't.

There is no order to the cards. You can't see the cards, so you have no idea what order they are in. A new player might make the hands better or worse or not change anything at all—because a new player has no control over anything.

Those two cards are a 50-50 event at the end of the round. The dealer will either bust, or he'll make it to 21.

The Superstition: *Always stand on a soft hand such as A:5 because if you hit or double, it will get worse.*

The Truth: Continuing with the above scenario, you are now at third base. The dealer is still showing his 6. You can take a hit or double down (doubling is the right move). The two cards to come out are still a 5 and a 10, but we don't know what order they are in. Will doubling help or hurt you?

It's a 50-50 proposition again.

If you double (or hit), you can get the 10. You would stand on your 16 against the dealer's 6. The dealer will hit his 16, get the 5, and you lose. Or, you double; you get the 5 and make it to 21. The dealer hits his 16, gets a 10 and busts. You win.

Let us say that you do nothing. You stand with your A:5. What then? It's still 50-50. The dealer will beat you half the time and half the time the dealer will bust.

The Superstition: *Picture cards always follow picture cards. If you've just seen a picture card, don't hit your stiff hand.*

The Truth: In a deck of 52 cards, 16 of them are picture cards (we count the 10 here), so that is 31 percent of the deck. If you have seen two picture cards, the percent of the deck is now down to 28 percent. There are fewer picture cards remaining. Hitting a stiff hand (12, 13, 14, 15, 16) is now actually a better proposition for you.

This superstition is harmful to you if you follow it.

The Superstition: *Never hit a 12, because you will always bust.*
The Truth: Some people feel that the 12 "brings out the 10s" and they must stand on all 12s or stand on 12 against the dealer's 2. The likelihood is that a non-10 card is next is always greater than the likelihood that a 10-valued card is next. Only 31 percent of as deck is composed of 10s.

This superstition is harmful to you if you follow it.

The Superstition: *You should play your hands differently, depending upon whether the table is running hot or cold.*
The Truth: There are definitely streaks in blackjack—good streaks, bad streaks, choppy streaks. You can lose 20 hands in a row, as I once did, or you can win 20 hands in a row. However, when someone experiences a losing streak, the person right next to him can be experiencing a winning streak. The person next to her can be breaking even. Good, bad, and indifferent streaks are not predictable. Yes, there are times when the dealer makes every bust hand into 20 and 21. There are times when the dealer busts like wild. Unfortunately, there is no way to predict when the busts will come or when the hits will come.

Speed Counters have slightly more insight into the probabilities in the remaining deck or decks because in high counts there are more 10-valued cards remaining than normal. In low counts, there are fewer 10-valued cards remaining. But that does not translate into perfect predictability, just a better probability.

In short, if you are a traditional Basic Strategy player, do not change the way you play your hands because of the recent streaks you or the dealer have been experiencing.

The Superstition: *A player at third base should always take the dealer's bust card.*
The Truth: I really wish that were an option. The player can volunteer to bust out the rest of us. But it isn't an option, as the first superstition shows us.

The Superstition: *I just lost 10 hands in succession, so I'm due to win the next hand.*

The Truth: You just lost those 10 hands, and now you are in the position of the third baseman in the A-5 example previously. Are you guaranteed a win on the next round? No, you aren't. You have a 50-50 chance of winning and a 50-50 chance of losing. Your streak has a 50-50 chance of ending and a 50-50 chance of continuing.

The Superstition: *Changing the dealer will cause me to lose.*

The Truth: Why? Will the new dealer change the order of the cards, the order of which no one on earth knows? The change of the dealer has no effect on anything, unless the dealer is a card mechanic brought in to cheat you. That is unlikely to happen.

If the new dealer is nasty, it might not be as pleasant playing with that dealer. But it has nothing to do with blackjack. That has to do with emotions, and although emotions count, they don't count cards.

The Superstition: *Bringing in new cards will cause me to lose.*

The Truth: If you have been on a hot streak, you fear the new cards will cool you off. If you have been on a cold streak, what then? Will everything get hot? The new cards have nothing to do with anything, except they smell better than the old cards, are crisper, and have less hand grease on them.

The Superstition: *Play at a blackjack table only where the dealer is cold.*

The Truth: The dealer might have been as cold as Alaska in winter for the last hour or day or week. You sit down and there is no guarantee that the dealer will remain cold. Winter always ends, even in Alaska.

The Superstition: *You must be a mathematical genius to win.*

The Truth: You have learned Speed Count and the OBS. You are now playing with an edge over the house—are you a genius? You might be, but that has nothing to do with your ability to beat the casinos at blackjack.

The Superstition: *You need a tremendous bankroll to win tremendous amounts of money.*

The Truth: How do you make a small fortune in Las Vegas? You start with a large fortune. Bahda-bing!

Basic Strategy players can be billionaires. So what? Unfortuately, in the long run they will lose. Speed Counters using proper bankroll-sizing techniques in accord with Risk of Ruin calculations, yes, to win a lot must have a large bankroll. And, yes, to win large sums, you must bet large sums. But for the average Basic Strategy player and even the average ploppy, the question is: How do you make a small fortune in Vegas? I'm sure you can guess the answer now.

The Superstition: *The objective of blackjack is to get to 21.*
The Truth: No, no, no, the objective of blackjack is to beat the dealer. You can beat the dealer with a 12! Twenty-one is merely the highest level of card attainment before you go bust. It is not the aim of the game. The aim, once again, is to beat the dealer.

The Superstition: *Betting progressions can overcome the house edge.*
The Truth: No. Sorry. Betting progressions can change the pattern of *how* you win and lose your money. In positive progressions, where you increase your bet when you win a hand, you will have many more losses because you are not collecting your full win on the bets. However, you will have some spectacular sessions when you win many hands in a row and get those bets to the sky.

In negative progressions, where you increase your bets when you lose a hand, you will have many more small winning sessions and a few spectacular losing sessions when you increase, lose, increase, lose, increase lose and you ultimately get to table max—and lose again!

In the long run, you will lose the house edge on the totality of the money you wager. That's the fact behind this superstition.

The Superstition: *Always insure a good hand.*
The Truth: If you have two 10s and the dealer has an ace as his up-card, is it more or less likely that he will have a 10 in the hole to give him a blackjack? It is less likely because you have taken two 10-valued cards out of play. For Speed Counters, there are insurance hands when the count gets to certain levels at the various games. Otherwise, the

house has a nice fat edge on this bet—whether you have a good hand or a bad hand.

The Superstition: *Taking even money guarantees that you will win.*
The Truth: This is a "true" superstition that costs you money at the game. "Even money" is just another name for insurance. The dealer shows an ace, you have a blackjack and you take the one-to-one payoff rather than gamble that the dealer doesn't have a blackjack. This is a bad decision. The dealer has only an approximately 30 percent chance to have a 10 in the hole, because you have taken one 10 out of play. So 30 percent of the time you will win even money on your blackjack when the dealer also has a blackjack. The other 70 percent of the time you also win just even money, instead of 3-to-2.

Now if you didn't insure, you would break even on the 30 hands that the dealer had a blackjack. But on 70 percent of the hands, you would win 3-to-2. You make more money not taking even money!

The Superstition: *You have to have a photographic memory to count cards in the casino.*
The Truth: Traditional card counting does not require a photographic memory—it requires you to remember a lot of elements as explained earlier in this book, and none of these elements have to do with remembering the card pictorially.

The Superstition: *Card Counters have a big advantage in blackjack tournaments.*
The Truth: Tournament blackjack is a whole different game than counting cards in a normal game against the house. In tournaments you are playing against your fellow players. There will be times you must bet big to catch someone, and it doesn't matter what the count is at these times. In protecting a lead, there may be times when you bet small—even if the count is sky high. Card counting is not necessary to be a good tournament player.

The Superstition: *It's impossible to win at blackjack; it is a game of luck.*

The Truth: Actually, this isn't a superstition but a statement of fact for almost all blackjack players. Although playing correct Basic Strategy will cut that house edge down to a minimum, the house will still have a small edge over you. The math of the game (math = luck) will dictate that the players lose in the long run. Those of you playing Speed Count will be the exceptions to this truth. You will have the edge over the house and the luck (math) will favor you in the long run.

CHAPTER 15
Winning Blackjack Tournaments

Blackjack tournaments allow players to compete against other players rather than against the casino. You and your opponents start with the same bankroll and play a set number of hands, and a player with the most chips after the round is over wins and advances to play other table winners. The initial large field of players is eventually whittled down to six or seven finalists, who play a final round to determine the tournament champion. The player who finishes in first place receives the lion's share of the prizes, while the other finalists receive various cash prizes.

The main goal of tournament play is to end up with more chips than your opponents. You could have a starting bankroll of 1,000 chips and wind up with only 100 chips but still advance if your fellow table players have fewer than 100 chips. Yes, you are still playing your hand against the dealer's hand, but you've got to keep an eye on your opponents' bankrolls so that you know if you are ahead or behind and then bet accordingly. Obviously, if you are leading, you want to protect your lead. If you are behind, you want to try to bet more to catch up and pass the leaders. How best to go about this will be discussed shortly, but for now let's review the different formats used in blackjack tournaments.

Types of Blackjack Tournaments

Traditional Elimination Tournaments: This is probably the most popular format. In these tournaments, you are playing only against the players on your table, with the table winners advancing and the others eliminated. In most elimination tournaments, you can pay a rebuy fee and continue to play.

Non-Elimination or Accumulation Tournaments: Here you compete against all the other players in the tournament with the goal of trying to win the most chips after several rounds. The tournament leaders are often posted on a "leader board" so all players have an idea of how much they need to win to overtake the leaders.

Tournaments with Elimination Hands: The player with the lowest chip count after hands 8, 16, and 25 is eliminated from play.

Live-Money Tournaments: In most tournaments, the playing chips have no value. But in live-money tournaments, players must purchase the chips, and they can be exchanged for cash at the end of the tournament. So in live-money tournaments, if you decide to go all-in and wager the maximum bet, that's your own money that you are putting at risk.

Mini Tournaments: These tournaments are usually held on a weekly and sometimes daily basis. They have a relatively low entry fee and take less than a day to complete. The prize pool is usually $2,000, sometimes a little more and sometimes a little less.

Major Tournaments: These tournaments have higher entry fees, generally take more than one day to complete, and have a sizeable prize pool. Casinos that offer major tournaments usually hold them over a weekend, offer the contestants free or discounted rooms, and usually include a banquet and free gift.

Sit-n-Goes: These are continuously running tournaments that begin when six players have been assembled. Sit-n-Goes are popular on Internet sites that offer blackjack tournaments, and a few brick-and-mortar casinos have also offered them.

Wild-Card Drawings: In some tournaments, names of players who were eliminated in early rounds go into a drum from which several names are randomly selected, and these wild-card winners get to play again in the semifinal and sometimes final round. This is a nice perk, and there have been many tournaments that have been won by players who were wild-carded.

Some tournaments are by invitation only. This is one way that casinos can reward their loyal customers; namely by inviting them to a special tournament where they have the chance to win a lot of money. If you are a steady customer at one or more casinos, check with the marketing department or with a casino host about being invited to invitational blackjack tournaments.

Blackjack tournaments are popular in casinos for the following reasons:
- You don't have to have the edge over the house to be successful in tournaments.
- Your advantage in tournaments arises from being a better tournament player than your opponents.
- The payoff for a small initial investment can be astronomical.
- You limit your losses to the amount of the entry fee.

Playing Format: In tournaments, players rotate betting. At the start of each round, the dealer will determine which player will make the first bet on the first hand by some random method. In some tournaments they deal a five-card poker hand to each player, and the player who has the highest poker hand bets first. In other tournaments, they roll a die, and the number rolled designates which player bets first. For example, if the player seated in betting spot No. 3 is first to bet, a rotating disk or marker is placed in front of player No. 3 to indicate that he is first. Usually the marker will have the number *1* on it to signify it is the first hand in the round.

Every player must bet in turn, starting with player No. 3. After the first hand is completed, the dealer will place a marker with No. 2 on it in front of the player in seat four. This player then gets to bet first with all the other players waiting until it's their turn to make their bet. By rotating the betting, every player has the chance to bet first or, more important, last.

Betting Rules: There are three important rules to remember when it comes to betting in tournaments.

First, wait until it's your turn to make a bet (i.e. don't place your chips in the betting circle until it's your turn). Second, string bets are not allowed. This means you are not allowed to take a pile of chips in your hand and then drop some of them one at a time into the betting spot. Nor can you place some chips in the betting spot then go back and add more chips. You should decide how many chips you want to bet, stack those chips outside of your betting spot, and then slide them into the spot.

Third, in tournament play you must stack your tournament chips in front of you by denomination or color. This makes it easier for every player to gauge how much bankroll opponents have as the round progresses.

In most tournaments there will be a *countdown* of players' chips, usually five hands before the last hand. In a tournament that consists of 30 hands, play will stop after hand 25, and the dealer along with a floor supervisor, will count and announce each player's bankroll. This process is repeated at the end of the round to determine the table winner(s).

Neither will you be allowed to bring strategy cards or other papers with you when you play and are not allowed to speak with any spectators or get advice from anyone as to how much to bet or how to play your hands. These rules are enforced, and there have been instances where a player was disqualified from a tournament for violating them.

Determine the Tournament's Equity: Players must pay an entry fee to play in a tournament. The best tournaments are those that return all the tournament entry fees in prizes to the players. In some tournaments, the casino might even kick in some more money to fund the prize pool. These are the most desirable tournaments.

The least desirable tournaments are those where the prize pool is less than the entry fees. But keep this in mind: Even though a casino might pay out less, it might also give players free rooms, free meals, and other perks, so you need to factor the value of these perks in to the equation.

Please Note: *Compare the prize pool plus the value of the tournament perks to the total entry fees to be sure the former is close to, or ideally slightly greater than, the latter.*

Read the Tournament's Rules: When you enter a tournament, read the tournament playing rules, because no two tournaments have exactly the same rules. I've seen many players make costly playing mistakes because they simply didn't take the time to read the written rules.

You can usually get a copy of the tournament rules after signing up for a tournament, or at a minimum, you will be given a set of rules just prior to playing. Take the time to read the rules so you know what the betting limits are, whether or not each player's bankroll is counted a few hands prior to the last hand, how many hands are played, how many players advance, whether surrender is allowed, and in the case of tournaments with elimination hands, which ones they are. If you have any questions, ask the folks running the tournament before you sit down and play.

The 13 Tournament Skills: There is a set of tournament skills that often determines whether or not a player will succeed in tournament play. Don't be overwhelmed when you read them here, because I'll be giving you some tips shortly that will help you master some of these skills.

1. Keeping track of the chip count of other players. You won't know how much to bet if you don't know the bankrolls of your opponents.
2. Knowing when it's best to go for the high (betting enough so that if everyone wins, you have the highest chip count).
3. Knowing when it is best to go for the low (keeping the most chips so that if everyone loses, you still have the most chips).
4. Knowing when to *correlate* (bet the same as your opponent's bet).
5. Knowing when to increase your bet.
6. Knowing when to bet the opposite of your opponents or simply bet the minimum.
7. Being able to mentally determine the outcome of a player's bet— what his bankroll will be if he wins, loses, or pushes his hand.
8. Knowing how to lock out an opponent so no matter what the outcome of the hand, you will advance.
9. Knowing the importance of betting position. Betting first in an elimination or final hand puts you at a distinct disadvantage compared to betting last.
10. Knowing when and how to deviate from the Basic Strategy.

11. Knowing how and when to use *secret bets* and *action cards* in tournaments that have them.
12. Knowing how to use the surrender rule in tournaments that offer surrender.
13. Knowing how to bet aggressively in tournaments that have elimination rounds.

Tournament Playing and Betting Strategy Tips: As soon as it is determined who is betting first on the first round, figure out what betting position you will have on the last round. If you are going to be "on the button" on that important last hand, you should bet more aggressively during the tournament to try to get the lead going into the last hand.

Keep in mind that if players bust out during the round, the position of the last button will change. If you fall behind a leader, it's best to make one or two large bets to try to catch up rather than a series of medium-sized bets. Wait for the dealer button to pass you before you make your large bet.

Another way to catch up to a leader is to bet the opposite. If he bets big, you bet small or vice versa. But if you fall more than a max bet behind and it's past the midpoint of the tournament, consider making large bets to catch up or at least get close to the leader.

If you are the chip leader, it's best to match the amount wagered by your nearest competitors, making it more difficult for them to catch you. Also, if your nearest opponent stands on a stiff, you should also do the same (you want to correlate).

You should practice *chip counting* so you can estimate your opponent's bankroll going into those last few crucial hands. Purchase some inexpensive clay casino chips of different denominations, stack them at home, and estimate the amount of money in each stack. Players who learn how to count chips accurately have a big edge in blackjack tournaments. Some good tournament players can actually keep track of the bankrolls of their opponents in their heads during the last few hands so they know for sure exactly how much they are ahead or behind and can then make the optimum bets.

You should try to get the lead prior to the last hand. If that means you have to bet big a few hands prior to the last hand, then do so even if it means busting out.

Pay attention to the maximum betting limit. You don't want to be more than one max bet behind the leaders going into the last couple of crucial hands. Otherwise, you won't be able to bet enough to catch them. You should have enough chips to double down or pair split.

Your betting position is also important. A contender who bets last on the last hand has a big edge over one who has to bet first. You must also be ready to pair split or double down on the last hand if necessary to win enough money to take the lead.

·   If you don't have enough chips to catch the leader, then hold back one more chip than the leader, bet the rest, and then hope that the dealer beats the table. This is known as going for the low.

If several opponents in a qualifying round bet it all on the last hand or you believe they will if they bet after you and you plan to do the same, then hold back one chip. If the dealer beats the table, you might possibly end up in second place and advance because you held back one chip while they busted.

If you need to make a large bet toward the critical last few hands, consider betting half your bankroll. This gives you the option of pair-splitting if you draw a pair. Unlike doubling down, you can't pair-split for less, which is why you bet half your bankroll and have the other half in reserve to pair-split or double down.

Please Note: *You are in a tournament to win. Often playing aggressively is the only choice you have, so never be afraid of busting out.*

CHAPTER 16

Three Radical Strategies

The information in this chapter deals with three new or relatively unknown advantage-play strategies at blackjack. I have used each one, and I can tell you that they work. None of these are requirements for being an advantage player, as most blackjack card counters never use them or in fact have never heard of them. But they are interesting to read about and fun to execute.

The Fat Finger Technique

For several years some Las Vegas casinos offered a double-deck game dealt face up. This was unusual, because most double-deckers are dealt face down. You will probably find some casinos throughout the country that continue to do the face-up double-deck game, and if so, the Fat Finger Technique can give you a startlingly large edge.

As a Speed Counter, the ultimate spot on the table is at first base, and this is the spot where the Fat Finger Technique works best.

The dealer deals the cards to the players face up. When the dealer gets to third base and he starts to flip the card over for the player, there are times when he double flips—that is, he starts to flip two cards at the same time. Then, knowing he was about to show his hole card, he quickly stops the flip and fixes the cards so the player gets the correct card without the dealer's hole card being seen or being flipped.

That hole card is often visible from first base. That's right; he isn't able to hide the card completely from the first-base player—who is you! Now you know his hole-card and can play your hands with that knowledge.

What makes this a great way to play for an OBS player is the fact that you have already made some unorthodox hitting, doubling, and standing decisions, so when you hit your 17 against the dealer's 8 up-card, the pit will think it is another bonehead play. He will not know that you know the dealer has a 10 in the hole and that your only choice is to hit your hand.

The reason I call this the Fat Finger Technique simply has to do with what dealers tend to make this misstep. These are usually large guys with big, thick fingers. For some reason, when they flip the cards, they have a tendency to double-card flip. That double-card flip is no big deal when it occurs to the players before the last player, but when it is the last player being double-card flipped—voilá, there is a nice fat edge for you.

Yes, at times all types of dealers have made this mistake, but the large, thick-fingered ones make it the most.

The best dealer I ever had did it about 5 to 10 percent of the time. I didn't go all out to take hits. If I had an 18 or 19 I stayed even though I knew the dealer had, say, a 20. That would have been too radical a hit.

I did, however, double down on hands against a dealer's 10 up-card when I knew he had a small card in the hole. This merely looked as if I were stupid as opposed to hitting on an 18 or 19, which would have made me look crazy.

I played these face-up two-deck games for more than a year, and it was a very, *very* satisfying year indeed.

The Grifter's Gambit, or, Inverse Hand-Spreading

The Grifter, a gifted advantage player in blackjack, has come up with a betting strategy for high counts called the Grifter's Gambit, which was published in Henry Tamburin's newsletter, *The Blackjack Insider*. He cites two other sources for this technique—Mason Malmuth for recommending it in single-deck games in his book *Blackjack Essays* (1985) and George C. for doing extensive simulations of it. Grifter has extended its use to double-deck and good six-deck games.

The technique refers to reversing the normal card counter's strategy of spreading to more hands as the count becomes advantageous for the player and instead playing fewer hands at much higher stakes. In the Grifter's Gambit, you start by playing three small-bet hands and reduce to one *much larger* bet hand as the count increases. (You can use two initial hands as well.) This method can be applied to any card-counting system.

Dan Pronovost's simulations show that this method indeed works as the Grifter documented. So with Dan's imprimatur, the Grifter's Gambit is an interesting strategy to use.

How does it work in the casino?

As all counters know, the basic principle of card-counting systems is to track the player's advantage or disadvantage with the casino, and simply bet more when the odds are in your favor and less when the casino is the favorite. All winning card-counting systems can be boiled down to this simple principle, regardless of the method they use to track the player's advantage.

A common method of getting more bets out when the advantage is very high in the player's favor is to play more than one hand with a large bet. Because this is commonly known as "hand-spreading," we'll refer to the Grifter's Gambit as "inverse hand-spreading."

To understand inverse hand-spreading, let's look at a typical betting system in a common six-deck game:

If you are playing $5 on three spots, the Speed Count goes to 34 or higher, and your betting range is one to eight, you will have $120 in total action riding during such a count. That total bet is spread out over three hands, which means $40 per hand. Your increases in bets could follow this pattern:

- Six-deck game
- Unit bet size: $5
- Playing three hands
- Count 30 or under, three hands of $5 each
- Count 31: three hands of $10 each
- Count 32: three hands of $15 each
- Count 33: three hands of $20 each
- Count 34 or more: three hands of $40 each

Now to establish the correct inverse hand-spread, we need to determine our bets and hands so that the total amount bet at each true count is almost the same as the above setup. Done this way, we should end up with similar variation and risk in each game, with comparable results. Assuming we want to start with three hands, we can use the following inverse spread:

- Six-deck game
- Unit bet size: $5
- Playing three hands down to one hand as the count increases
- Count: 30 or under, three hands of $5=$15 (three hands of one unit)
- Count: 31 or 32, three hands of $10=$30 (three hands of two units)
- Count: 33: two hands of $30=$60 (two hands of six units)
- Count: 34 or more: one hand of $120 (one hand of 24 units)

With this setup, we are betting almost the same total amount at each count level. Notice that we had to use a unit bet size in the inverse single-hand game that is three times larger than the inverse spread unit bet size. This is a requirement if you are trying to match the performance metrics between the two systems. It also makes clear that inverse hand-spreading requires players to have an equivalent unit bet size three times higher than the table minimum. For example, if you are a $10 player playing at $10 tables, then using an equivalent inverse spread is not possible without tripling your bankroll risk. Inverse hand-spreading is not suitable for players whose unit bet size is at or near table minimums.

What Dan discovered in his simulations was interesting. In six-deck games, inverse hand-spreading actually outperformed normal increases that advantage blackjack players usually make. That means you actually win more money. In two-deck games the reverse was true. Normal increases at different counts tended to outperform inverse hand-spreading at those same counts.

Is this a valid technique? It certainly is. I've used it on occasion, and most pit bosses have never seen it before.

Must you formulate how you do it based on my examples above? No. If you play this technique, just bet according to your bankroll. Make your largest bet, whatever that may be, on that one big pile of chips.

Another good technique would be to mix it up. Hand-spread sometimes; inverse hand-spread at other times.

Hey, That's My Card!

Sometimes the dealer will hit a hand of a player incorrectly, either because the player did not signal for a hit but made some kind of gesture that the dealer mistook for a hit signal, or the dealer decided to play the player's hand—there are indeed some dealers who take it upon themselves to play out the common hands for the player before the player signals what he wants to do.

In cases where such a thing happens and you are the next to play your hand, then demand that the card given to the player before you be given to you, that is, if that card helps you. For example, if you have a 12 and the player before you is mistakenly given a 9, you want that 9 for your own hand. In fact, not only do you want that 9, but you want to double on that 9 so you get a 21!

The worst that can happen is the floor person won't allow it. But if the dealer doesn't allow it, demand that the floor person be brought over and explain that the card is yours and that if it is discarded it screws up "the order of the cards." By showing how stupid you are about such a thing as "the order of the cards" you have a nice shot that the floor person will allow you to take that card.

The reverse should also be done. If the card mistakenly given to the player before you is a card that hurts you or makes your hand a poor one—such as any bust hand or a 17 or 18, then tell the dealer, "I don't want that card. It isn't mine. It belongs to the player before me. Give me a new card." Again, if the dealer hesitates or tries to bully you into taking the card, make him call over the floor person.

CHAPTER 17

Frequently Asked Questions for Advantage Players

I am going to bring in the experts for this chapter to give you their opinions concerning various advantage-play topics. So you'll be hearing from expert blackjack player and best-selling author Henry Tamburin, expert card counter Dominator, and Dan Pronovost—the man for all blackjack seasons. Yes, I'll have some comments too.

Question: *Should advantage players tip the dealers?*
Henry Tamburin: If you are a $10 Golden Touch Blackjack player, your expectation is to win close to $9 per hour. This profit can be easily negated by overtipping. However, if your dealer is friendly and makes your playing session enjoyable, and you want to tip for good service, here's a way to do it that will save you money. Place a dollar chip on top of your chips in the betting circle and tell the dealer, "This is for you." If the hand wins, give the dealer the winning dollar chip and let the original dollar chip ride on the next hand. As long as you keep winning, so will the dealer. Tipping in this manner will also give you a slightly higher average bet for rating purposes. Quarter and black-chip Golden Touch Blackjack players have higher win rates, so they can afford to tip more ($5 tip bet is suggested).

In fact, tipping at that betting level is good camouflage, because the casino's stereotype of a card counter is someone who never tips. You will also be increasing your average bet and comps. In casinos where dealers have some leeway in where they position the cut card after the shuffle (i.e. the penetration), a tip now and then might also influence them to position that cut card slightly deeper than normal. Timing a tip can also help. If the count is high and a relief dealer arrives at the table, making a tip bet for your dealer might influence her to deal out one more hand before relinquishing the cards to the relief dealer.

Dominator: Many card counters have this thing about not tipping, as if tipping is bad. There are many careers where tips are the main salary ingredient—waiters, waitresses, barbers, maids, valet parkers, and also dealers. If the dealers were paid a living wage, the cost of the games would go up and you would not have any $10 tables left. A small tip for a good dealer should be factored into your playing scheme.

Frank Scoblete: I tip good dealers. It's their livelihood and a reward for good service. However, $5 players have to be very careful about tipping because their edge is small. But if you are a $25 or $100 player, then by all means, give some tips each half hour.

Question: *I have trouble keeping the count; help me!*
Frank Scoblete: Some people do have trouble keeping the count in the noisy casinos—especially when they first begin playing as an advantage player. Don't fret. There's an easy way to keep the count, which I will explain to you shortly. But first, what usually makes someone forget the count are other numbers in your head competing with the Speed Count number—like adding up the hands of the other players and the dealer and putting those numbers in your head. If you put the numbers for the hands they are playing in your head next to your Speed Count number, you can easily forget the Speed Count. So that's my first piece of advice. Forget playing the game of blackjack for the other players and the dealer. You have to play your own hands, but the other people at the table are irrelevant. You don't play their hands. You just do the Speed Count.

You can keep the count with your chips. Make sure you have several piles of chips in front of you—and make sure those piles are composed of chips of all colors. You'll want some $1 chips too—maybe 10 to 20 of them. Have some of the chips spilling over. You want to be a little bit of a pig here.

One pile of the few in front of you is your counting pile. If you are playing a double-deck game, you can have a green chip with a red one on top. That is your initial count of 30. When the next round is finished you can add ones to that pile if the count went up or take off the red chip and add ones to give you the numbers 26, 27, 28, 29. You can even have a couple of reds under the green chip to make this pile look as messy as the other piles. Indeed, if you have four reds under the green chip and the count should dip under 25, you can take the green chip off. When those cards are being dealt out, you can fiddle with your chips because you aren't interested in other people's draws. What you *don't want* in front of you are several piles of neatly stacked chips with each denomination being its own pile and then you have that one messy one with different colors. That looks weird and might even look suspicious.

Sometimes if you have played too long, your mind can get fuzzy and you'll find yourself daydreaming and losing the count. That is the time to quit the session and take a walk or a nap.

Henry Tamburin: When you practice at home, you should have a noisy environment to simulate what happens in the casinos. That can be helpful to you. The casino atmosphere does not make it easy to think. They don't want you to think. So mimic that in your practice sessions.

Question: *Is it wise to play with other card counters at the same table?*
Dominator: I hate to ride the fence with this question, but the answer is yes and no. First let us talk about why this isn't a good idea. When two Speed Counters are at the same table, chances are that both of you will be increasing your bets at the same time, and worse, by the same amount. This can look very suspicious to the pit critters. The beauty of Speed Count is not only the simplicity of the system but also that you will be making bets sooner than a normal Hi-Lo card counter would. But two people increasing their bets at the same time just isn't a good idea.

If you are going to play with other Speed Counters at the same table, you should not bet the same ways. You must vary how you spread your bets so you don't look as if you are following the same script. We use a way of betting that allows us to move bets around in low counts so our players are never betting the same way. My minimum bet might be $100, but I will bet $80 or $110 or $75 or $95, while my friend will bet $100,

$75, $95, or $110. You mix it up. Also in high counts, you never want to peak your bets at the same level. It is more dangerous to play with other card counters at the tables, and you might want to give yourselves only a half hour at any one table doing this.

Frank and I will play together at the same table as a team. But before we start, we have a predefined method of increasing our bets as I have shown. We also have a predefined way of acting at the tables that will throw off the pit critters. So if you want to play with a card counter, you must have a plan and stick to it as you play.

Frank Scoblete: You are better never playing at tables with other card counters—it tends to bring attention to the table with everyone raising their bets at the same time. That's not too obvious! You might be doing just fine, but the other counter brings the attention, and an accident catches you too. It is best, when all is said and done, to play without other counters at the table. Of course, I have played with other counters at the table using Dominator's advice above. But you must be very careful even with other Speed Counters at the same table.

Henry Tamburin: I stay away from other counters when I play. Many counters give out too many signals that they are keeping track of the cards.

Question: *I know that Frank has many tricks in craps to increase one's average bet without the monetary risk involved. Are there any comp tricks for blackjack?*

Frank Scoblete: As an advantage blackjack player, you are playing with an edge over the casino. Let us say you are playing with a half-percent edge over the house. You win 50 cents for every $100 you bet. However, the casino rates you as losing $2 for every $100 you bet because most casinos traditionally figure blackjack players to be facing a 2 percent house edge. The casino will return about 40 percent of your loss in the form of comps. So you get 80 cents in comps for every $100 you bet. Let us say you are a $10 Speed Counter. The casino will rate you as playing about $20 per hand (remember they figure your increases in high counts as part of your betting), and if you play about 100 hands an hour, that's $2,000 in action. You win $10 per hour from your edge. You also get $16 per hour in comps. As a $10 Golden Toucher you are now winning $26 from the casinos every hour. If you are a $50 player, just multiply these figures by five.

Here is some more information, slightly borrowed from *Casino Craps: Shoot to Win!* by Dominator and me.

The casinos have staffs of expert psychologists, psychiatrists, and public-relations people hunkering in underground bunkers where they figure out ways to fuel the players' desire to be loved, appreciated, and desired. These "psychos" are expert at making gamblers bet more, play more, lose more—and seemingly enjoy it more. And all the casino bosses, shareholders, and executives laugh at the foolish gamblers trying to overcome Lady Luck's capriciousness. And the money rolls in!

Okay, that paragraph was a little over the top. Most of the "psychos" are actually above ground. The rest of that paragraph is thematically true, if not also literally true.

The casinos beat gamblers with the house edge on their games, with their massive bankrolls, and with their ability to get the players to almost enjoy throwing their money away. One of the best tools in the casinos' psychological warfare with the players is in the area of comps—those supposed freebies given to loyal players. Comps are the biggest weapon in getting people to gamble more than they want and sometimes more than they ought.

Comps are used to make casino gamblers want to be recognized, loved, appreciated, lionized, and revered. All those red-chip players look at the comps of the green-chip players and are envious. Green-chip players look at black-chip players and are envious. Black-chip players look at purple-chip players who are looking at orange-chip players who are looking at gold-chip players who are looking at brown-chip players who are looking at (the late) Kerry Packer, who was treated as a god—and everyone wishes to be worshipped like that.

The big room, food, and beverage (RFB) comps—that is, comps for everything: your room, food, drinks, shows, limos, shopping sprees, and exclusive parties—are the nectar of the gambling gods, and even the lowliest player wishes to partake.

And how dopey is that? Completely and utterly.

Comps are meaningless if you are losing your money to the casino. So what if they are giving some of your money back to you in the form of comps? You are still a loser. But for some unfathomable reason, casino gamblers are in love with comps. They think, perhaps, that comps tell them something important about themselves, when in fact the casino would comp a bum who bet and lost enough to "merit" it. In fact, in a past book of mine is the true story of the "million dollar bum" who received incredible comps while on a winning streak at Treasure Island (now called TI). The casino personnel escorted him to the street when he had lost it all.

Comps are a waste of time pursuing if they cost more to get than they return. If you are expected to lose $5,000 based on your level of betting, the fact that the casino might return $2,000 in the form of comps just means you are a $3,000 loser.

Let's go through how this works.

The formula for the monetary edge is simple: comps + win/loss = monetary edge. Most casinos will give back between 30 percent and 50 percent of your expected *theoretical loss* in the form of comps. Your theoretical loss is not your actual loss. On any given trip you can win and still be considered a loser—or you can lose much more than your theoretical loss as well.

The formula for comps: avg. bet x number of decisions per hour x number of hours you play x house edge = theoretical loss

Casinos will often rate blackjack players as losing about 2 percent of their total action.

Casinos love to use psychology against the players; it helps the bottom line. But players can also psych out the casinos in the comping game. We want the casinos to rate us as bigger bettors than we actually are and/or we want to get more comps than we actually have earned. Here are some helpful hints to achieve our goals:

1. Always tip on top of your bet, not in front of it. Keep that bet riding for dealers; never take it off or give it to them, but let them know that bet is theirs if you keep winning. By doing this, the bet counts as a part of your bet, increasing your average bet. If you tip any other way, the bet does not count as a part of your bet. Also, you are betting only a single bet that can win over and over again if you get on a hot streak. On other types of tips, the casino dealers take both the tip and the win down. To keep the dealers in action you

have to make tip after tip after tip. You are spending more this way and receiving no benefit.

2. Always ask for a comp at least 10 minutes before you plan to leave a table. Let the rater think he has kept you at the table longer than you planned to be there. That helps you look stupid.

3. The BIG bet ploy: If you want to occasionally put up a "show bet" that is substantially bigger than your normal starting bet to get that in your rating, then do it while the dealer is shuffling. It will be up longer, seen more readily by the rater, and not be at risk until the hand. Sometimes if the rater goes to another table, you can even take the bet down—and have no risk and a nice rating.

4. If you are a "marginal RFB/room plus limited food and beverage (RLFB)" and you are staying at a property, do not put everything on your room and wait until the end to find out what it will comp. Instead—*comp as you go*. Many times you will be able to get café and buffet comps up front and then get the total theoretical loss at the end of your stay to put against your gourmet food as well.

5. If you have stopped playing and have asked for a comp, stay at the table. Let them ask you to move. The fact that you are taking up a space will motivate "the computer" to work faster on your comps.

6. If you are an RFB player and are interested in getting airfare for your play but have been turned down in the past, ask the casino to put you in a regular room and not a suite. Usually the suites are 5 to 10 times more expensive. If you stay in a regular room, you might reduce what the casino figures it has spent on you, and it just might give you your airfare.

7. The "Casino Psychology Departments" use comps as a way to *get you* to measure your "self-worth" based on how many comps you get and what a big shot you are for getting them. No comp is worth the loss of money or sleep. Play your game, and the comps will come or they won't. Use our tricks, too, because they can't hurt!

Dominator: Frank gives great advice about comps, but when all is said and done, you are playing to beat the house. The comps will come, or they won't come. Your main aim is to be an advantage player.

Question: *Don't the casino raters respect people who bet big?*

Dominator: Some casino players think that the size of their bets can get the casino personnel to think of them as big shots. Nothing could be further from the truth. Is it a smart person who plays a game where he must lose? I'd say no; that's pretty stupid behavior. Just betting bigger is even stupider behavior, because bigger bets mean bigger losses. Are the casino personnel really impressed by dopes willing to lose big money—even though these dopes get great comps that cost them a fortune in losses? I'd say the casino personnel are disdainful of such people. How can they be impressed by such stupidity?

Frank Scoblete: You play a game you can't beat, and you want respect for that? Are you crazy?

Question: *Can you explain the value of uneven betting?*

Henry Tamburin: Uneven betting is great camouflage that costs nothing. There are two types. Instead of betting, say, three green chips on one hand when the count increases, put out a rainbow of different-colored chips in your betting circle (like two greens, five reds, and a pink chip or some dollars). The latter looks a lot less onerous than three green chips. Fumbling around as you stack your rainbow also gives the perception that you don't know what you are doing. Another type of uneven betting that also is good camouflage is to bet uneven amounts when you spread to two hands. So instead of betting exactly two green chips on one hand and two greens on another hand when the count increases, bet uneven amounts (like $40 on one hand and $60 on the other hand). You are still betting a total of $100 on the two hands but in a manner that is not as traditional. Many card counters are too neat, and by being the opposite of neat, you will not look like a normal card counter.

Frank Scoblete: Uneven betting is great, and also being sloppy with your chips is great. These are the techniques of the ploppies, and they are wonderful for making you look less than what you are. If you play two hands, pretend that you are using some kind of progression betting, and always have more on one hand and less on the other hand.

Question: *You have mentioned it is a good thing to use the OBS cards at the table. Can you give me examples of why you think doing so is helpful?*
Dominator: I just love to tell this story about what actually happened to me at the tables because I always have the OBS card. Having the OBS card at the table with you always makes you look like a stupid player, and as a card counter, you want to look as stupid as you can get! Then, when a pit critter wants to look at the card and sees some of the plays that are different, you will get all sorts of comments like, "You don't know what you are doing."

Even better! Let me tell you that I have been called or thought of as a stupid player more than once, and I love it!

Now I will relate the ultimate "stupid" story. I am playing at a very well-known and popular Strip casino in Las Vegas. I am playing their shoe game when I get dealt an 8 and the dealer is showing a 6. So I take a look at my OBS card when it is my turn, and I put a double-down bet.

The dealer says to me, "Sir, are you sure that your card says to do that?"

I take another look at my card, use my fingers to go down the column and say, "Yes, it sure does!"

The dealer says to me, "Sir, where did you get that card because I have never seen that play before."

I just love when they ask me that, because I say, "Susan, I got this card from my grandfather. My grandfather brought this book over from Italy that had this blackjack strategy in it, and he always used it. Out of respect for my grandfather, I use it also. My grandfather always seemed to win, or at least that is what he told all of us."

The dealer gives me a shrug of her shoulders, deals me an ace, and I win my double down. Now the pit-critter lady comes over, not for anything more than just to watch the game, as the casino is dead, and I think she is bored. On the next shoe, I get dealt an ace-3 against the dealer's 4. I proceed to look at my card and proceed to put out my double-down bet. The pit lady says to me, "Sir, are you sure that your card says to do that?"

I don't have to answer, because the dealer says, "Oh yes, Linda, his card does say to do that. He got that card from his Italian grandfather."

Linda the pit critter says, "His grandfather should learn how to play blackjack!"

Now I am asking myself, should I act mad that Linda said that my grandfather, who never played blackjack in his life, didn't know how to play? Or should I just think that my camouflage is just so good and be happy they think me a complete idiot?

I wait until the end of the shoe to make my decision, and I can't resist. I call Linda over at the end of the shoe and say to her, "Linda, I want two apologies from you. First, you insinuate that I don't know how to play blackjack, and what difference does that make to you? Everyone at this table can bet their money any way they want to. But more important, you insulted my grandfather, a World War II veteran, even though he fought for Mussolini, and I want an apology!" At this point this little old man next to me, who didn't say one word as we were playing, says in a very strong Italian accent, "You betta apologize to his grandfather; I fought under Mussolini too!" The table went quiet, and the apology was given with me smiling to myself and saying, "Thank you, OBS!"

Question: *Are there any other betting methods that can camouflage what you are doing at the tables, which is betting more when you have the edge and less when the casino has the edge?*

Frank Scoblete: Here is a betting strategy that is excellent. It's called "go up and go down." The first round you start with your one unit and go to four units in a high count. If you get to four units, that's great. However, on the next round, you start at four units, and if the count becomes favorable, you stay at four units. If the count goes down, you drop your bet with the count. In this way, you are not always going one to four but also four to one. You mix up how you play the rounds so that your betting style is never easily discerned. Mixing up your betting like this is unusual, and very few card counters will do this.

Question: *Are casino coupons valuable? Can you go through some of the typical ones?*

Henry Tamburin: Yes, casino coupons are valuable, because you will always have the edge over the house when you use them. The most common are the matchplay, bonus blackjack, and free ace coupons. A matchplay coupon works like this. Suppose you have a $10 matchplay coupon. Place the matchplay coupon in the betting circle, and place $10 of your chips on top. If you win the hand, the casino will pay you $10 for your $10 wager and another $10 for the matchplay coupon. Essentially the casino doubled your payout if the hand wins (i.e. you bet $10 and won $20). Most matchplay coupons can be used for only one hand and win or lose, the casino will keep the coupon. The expected value of a $10 matchplay coupon is about $4.75 (probability of winning x face value of matchplay, or 47.5 percent x $10).

The bonus blackjack coupon pays a bonus on your first blackjack. Instead of the usual 3-2 payoff you will get paid 3-to-1 or 2-to-1. You will get a blackjack on average about once in every 21 hands. The expected value of a 3-to-1 coupon is the amount wagered x (1.5 – 21 x house edge). So if you wagered $25 with a 3-to-1 blackjack bonus coupon in a typical Las Vegas two-deck blackjack game where the house edge over the Basic Strategy player is 0.4%, the value of the coupon is $35.40 ($25 x [1.5 – 21 x 0.004]). Another valuable blackjack coupon is the "Free Ace," which substitutes as an ace for your first card. To use it, just place the coupon on the layout with a bet, and the dealer will skip over you the first time he deals around because your coupon represents an ace. If your next card is a ten or picture card, you automatically have a blackjack. These coupons usually specify the maximum amount you can wager along with the coupon (usually $5, $10, or $25). You have a big 55 percent edge using this coupon (assuming the free ace can be kept and replayed, which is usually the case—if it can't, your edge is 50.5 percent, which is also great).

Dominator: When you get coupons from certain magazines, it does peg you as a more intelligent player than most of the ploppies in the casino. You should just do coupon runs without playing in the casino where you are playing the coupon—at least not on that shift.

Frank Scoblete: In the past, you could play opposite propositions with coupons—for example, in craps you could bet a coupon on the Pass Line and your wife could bet her coupon on the Don't Pass line. Over the years casinos have become annoyed at this type of almost guaranteed win. So avoid being cute. Play the coupon properly. You really don't want to bring any attention to yourself.

Question: *What do they look for in the eye in the sky (EITS) to figure out if someone is counting?*

Henry Tamburin: All casinos have their own procedures, but in general the casino surveillance personnel in the EITS will first check if the player knows Basic Strategy. If the player doesn't, this might be enough for the EITS to determine the player is not a counter. The second characteristic the EITS looks for is how the player is moving his money. Does he always bet the same amount at the start of the shoe and then increase his bets as play progresses? Does he spread to two hands with fairly large bets, then drop to a smaller bet on one hand?

If they are still suspicious, the EITS will check if the player deviates from Basic Strategy. Most trained EITS personnel know about the hands that counters who use traditional counting systems will deviate from based on the count. One of the key hands they watch is a Hard 16. Counters will hit 16 when they bet small and stand on 16 when they bet large.

Some casinos also use sophisticated software, that allows them to determine if the player is a counter based on inputting how he plays and bets, or they will compare the player's facial characteristics to a casino database of known card counters. We do not change our bets based on the count. OBS improves our edge and makes us look somewhat stupid, and as Frank says, "Stupid is good."

Question: *When should I stop playing?*

Dominator: Our advice is to limit your playing time per session to about 45 minutes to one hour simply because the longer you play, the more time you give the casino to observe and analyze your playing characteristics. Other stopping points you might want to consider are after you spread to two (or more) hands with max bets at the end of the shoe or after you've gone through three to five cycles of your bet ramp. Staying too short a time is usually never a problem, but staying too long at the table can be.

Henry Tamburin: You might exit after a really good run that has brought attention to you. Say, "I'm taking this win home with me!" and leave the casino.

Frank Scoblete: No matter what—win or lose or break even—stop when you feel tired. If you start forgetting the count, it's time for a break.

Question: *What should you do if you have horrendous losing sessions?*
Henry Tamburin: If you've lost 10 percent or more of your total bank-roll, you should reevaluate your Risk of Ruin formula to determine if you need to lower your betting level. If you maintain the same betting level with a smaller bankroll, your Risk of Ruin might be too high. The Speed Count software is a good tool to help you determine this. What you should not do is get gun-shy and not bet the maximum when the Speed Count calls for it. Many beginning counters fall into this trap. You must load your gun with bullets (chips) and fire away when the edge shifts in your favor each and every time you play, otherwise you will never beat the game. You must also recognize the fact that you can lose when you have the edge. But overall you will increase your bankroll.

Frank Scoblete: Losing is part of the game. What I do when I lose is calmly go back to my room, curl up in the fetal position, and suck my thumb.

Dominator: I curse, yell, and scream, smoke a cigarette, and then I feel fine and I am ready to play again.

Dan Pronovost: I eat.

Question: *What should you do if you are playing a juicy two-deck game heads up, the count has skyrocketed, and a player walks up to the table ready to buy in?*
Henry Tamburin: When you are an advantage player, this is the worst possible time to have a new player join your game (assuming the casino allows mid-shoe entry, which it usually doesn't on $25 or higher games) because you will get fewer hands dealt in a favorable situation prior to the shuffle. One thing you can do to discourage the new player from entering is to say something to the effect of, "I hope you have a lot of money, 'cause Joe [the dealer] has been killing me." Most ploppies will heed your advice and move on. Another way to handle this situation is to simply ask the new player politely if he or she wouldn't mind waiting until after the shuffle before playing because you don't want to affect the

flow of the cards. Getting as many hands dealt when the Speed Count is high is important to maintain a healthy edge over the house.

Frank Scoblete: If you turn to the new player and show them you have drool coming from your mouth down your chin, dripping onto your shirt, and then you talk incoherently, "Blah, dung, carps, nutta," that will often send them running to a different table.

Dominator: I yell, curse, scream, and smoke a cigarette. That usually gets them to go to another table.

Question: *What should I do if the casino uses a six-deck shoe and cuts off half the decks?*
Dominator: Don't play. Your edge will be miniscule, so why bother? Head for the door and a new casino or, if you are on a boat, go up on deck and enjoy the view, even if it isn't so hot. Six-deck games with 50 percent penetration are a lot of work for very little return.

Dan Pronovost: I leave the casino and go have something to eat.

Question: *Can several players use the system as a team?*
Dominator: I enjoy team play with certain individuals, but you must be able to trust them to be honest. Most teams break up because several players get hot and win a lot of money and some players get cold and lose money, and the hot players don't like sharing their wins. You can read about team play in a lot of blackjack books, but it is a dangerous activity if the people are not trustworthy or if they are the suspicious types.

One way to play is to have what we call the "Opposite Gorilla." Most card-counting teams bring in a big player (or gorilla) to the table when the count is high. The big player bets big until the high count is over and then leaves. Casinos are thoroughly aware of this tactic and watch for it.

What Frank and my teams do is bring in a famous person, who sits down at the table and gives his or her card in, and the casino floor person is aware of who this person is. Sometimes other players come over and ask for this person's autograph. However, our famous players, while they will vary their bets to keep the pit interested, are really playing only Basic Strategy—at other tables in the high roller room or at high-end tables will be our team players. So much attention goes to our Opposite Gorilla that the other counters are free and clear to play pretty aggressively because all attention is on the famous person. Even when our famous players are sometimes asked not to play, which rarely happens, except in really paranoid casinos, that usually doesn't hurt the team because once the Opposite Gorilla leaves, the pit relaxes, thinking they have done a great job of protecting their games. In fact, the counters are hammering away at them for another hour or so. It's a great technique. Of course, you have to know famous people to have this work!

Frank Scoblete: Team play is fraught with problems, most of them regarding trust. In the beginning of your blackjack career, I think you should get down playing alone before you even think of playing in a team or forming a team.

Question: *Why don't you have index changes in the OBS like the other card-counting systems do?*

Dominator: Go into the corner, put this cap on, and listen up! The whole idea of Speed Count and OBS is for us to look *unlike* the other advantage players. Everything we are doing here is to give you freedom to play under the radar—as best as we can manage it. The OBS allows us to maximize our edge while still allowing us to play the same way hand after hand just like regular players. It makes us look worse than the average Basic Strategy player too. I will let you out of the corner if you listen to us carefully and follow our advice.

Frank Scoblete: The OBS is a brilliant way to play your hands. It increases your edge with Speed Count and makes you look dull.

CHAPTER 18

Speed Count Simulation Data: A Few Words from Dan Pronovost

Frank asked me to write up this technical section to fend off the few who demand, "More data! More proof! More sims!"

Inventing a new, simplified blackjack card-counting system is easy. Most well-known books include a passing section with some trimmed-down method usually titled something like, "A Really Useless Card-Counting System for Dummies, Because Losers Always Ask Me for One."

The results usually reflect the effort and authors' interest—poor. Professional blackjack card counters scoff at simplified strategies, because they have mastered something that clearly performs better. Anything less powerful is a waste of time, stupid, or a fraud. With such an attitude, it's no wonder the "easy" card-counting systems created to date have been virtually useless.

Professional players disdain average gamblers. I instead look at average gamblers, who play at a loss, as candidates in need of education, and in need of having something simple and fun instead of taxing.

As such, I spent a lot of time inventing and refining Speed Count to be as powerful as possible yet very easy to use. The hard part is not coming up with the card-counting method but proving it works and is easy to use in a pragmatic way.

So I modified my own company's blackjack simulator product, Blackjack Audit (cheap plug alert: www.HandheldBlackjack.com) to support the counting concept of Speed Count. No simulators at the time supported this, because the metric of counting cards per dealt hand was unheard of.

From there, I noodled with all kinds of variations of the method, counting low cards, high cards, tweaks for blackjacks, twists for dealer hands, etc. The result is what you see in this book, which I have gladly (for you *and* me) left for Frank to present to you, fine reader.

I ran billions and billions of simulations (actually about a trillion), testing all kinds of games and situations. Due to the unusual counting metric of Speed Count, I wanted absolute proof that the method would work well in different situations. What happens with more players, fewer players, more depth, different rules, more decks, fewer decks, etc.? And incredibly, Speed Count holds its own and works surprisingly well across the board!

Then I spent a lot of time refining the OBS, which is very much a give-and-take process requiring another mountain of simulations looking at very specific actions and hands.

Although there is a lot of data here, some critics will no doubt say it's not enough. To them I say, feel free to run extra simulations. Or, as Dominator says, "Feel free to go away!" Speed Count is a standard part of all our blackjack training products now, including our own simulator, Blackjack Audit, so anyone can replicate this data and complete more tests. Over time, I'm sure other simulators will be able to complete these tests, too. My goal in this section is to provide average players with content to help them understand how much money they will make in different games, the risk, the bankroll requirements, and the characteristics of Speed Count.

Details and Understanding the Tables

Behind every single row or result in the following tables is a simulation run of at least 100 million rounds. We used a $5 unit bet size, 75 percent penetration in all four-or-more-deck games, 67 percent penetration in all double-deck games, and 50 percent penetration in all single-deck games. Generally, we simulated all permutations of one and six players,

DAS/noDAS, S17-H17, 1-2-4-6-8 decks. This makes 2 x 2 x 2 x 5 = 40 different base simulations for everything we wanted to test.

These are reflected in the 40 rows you will tend to see over and over again in these tables. Other minor blackjack rules we assumed are:

- resplitting of aces allowed,
- no hitting split aces (one extra card only),
- up to two splits (three hands),
- dealer peeks for blackjack when dealt 10 up.

Win rate refers to the average number of bet units won per round dealt. To convert this into an hourly win rate, multiply by your unit bet size and expected rounds per hour, historically chosen to be 100.

Avg. bet refers to the average total wagers per round. This is slightly higher than the average bet size per hand, due to splits and doubles.

> **Please Note:** *We used a $5 unit bet size for all simulations. Simply multiply accordingly for higher unit bet sizes. It is important to know the difference between unit bet size and average bet size. A $10 player is one whose minimum bet size is $10, not his average bet size.*

SD: Abbreviation for the *standard deviation* per round of win/loss, per unit bet. Again, this is slightly different from the standard deviation per betting event or hand, due to splits and doubles. Standard deviation is a reflection of the variability of win or loss, or risk. A higher standard deviation means you will have more fluctuation in your bankroll as you play.

Exp.: Abbreviation for the *expectation* for this game. Expectation is the average amount of each bet you should expect to win back, over time. Not surprisingly, expectation times the average bet size will be the same as the win rate. When we quote an expectation value from a simulation, it is computed as the sum of all profit or loss divided by the sum of all bets. Some older blackjack books exclude splits and doubles from their expectation values, but we do not.

Conservative Speed Count Performance

PLAYERS	DECKS	DAS	H17	WIN RATE	AVG. BET	SD	EXP.
1	1	noDAS	H17	0.005606	$8.3430	1.90053	0.3360%
1	1	DAS	H17	0.007739	$8.4030	1.92113	0.4605%
1	1	DAS	S17	0.010180	$8.3560	1.90927	0.6091%
1	1	noDAS	S17	0.007995	$8.2900	1.88801	0.4822%
6	1	noDAS	H17	0.004743	$7.5700	1.72530	0.3132%
6	1	DAS	H17	0.006663	$7.6240	1.74352	0.4370%
6	1	DAS	S17	0.009000	$7.6050	1.73806	0.5918%
6	1	noDAS	S17	0.006953	$7.5330	1.71575	0.4615%
1	2	noDAS	H17	0.004720	$11.3370	2.74435	0.2082%
1	2	DAS	H17	0.007856	$11.4270	2.77863	0.3437%
1	2	DAS	S17	0.011103	$11.3090	2.75265	0.4909%
1	2	noDAS	S17	0.008139	$11.2270	2.72023	0.3625%
6	2	noDAS	H17	0.003479	$10.1790	2.50638	0.1709%
6	2	DAS	H17	0.006206	$10.2570	2.53680	0.3025%
6	2	DAS	S17	0.009420	$10.2090	2.52478	0.4614%
6	2	noDAS	S17	0.006701	$10.1360	2.49565	0.3305%
1	4	noDAS	H17	0.001893	$12.0630	3.02535	0.0785%
1	4	DAS	H17	0.005233	$12.1580	3.06474	0.2152%
1	4	DAS	S17	0.008715	$11.9260	3.01191	0.3654%
1	4	noDAS	S17	0.005487	$11.8400	2.97495	0.2317%
6	4	noDAS	H17	0.000772	$10.8450	2.75872	0.0356%
6	4	DAS	H17	0.003635	$10.9110	2.78984	0.1666%
6	4	DAS	S17	0.007267	$10.8260	2.76808	0.3356%
6	4	noDAS	S17	0.004449	$10.7640	2.73825	0.2067%
1	6	noDAS	H17	0.004085	$14.6060	4.30502	0.1398%
1	6	DAS	H17	0.007932	$14.7070	4.35944	0.2697%
1	6	DAS	S17	0.011992	$14.2470	4.24718	0.4209%
1	6	noDAS	S17	0.008253	$14.1580	4.19718	0.2915%
6	6	noDAS	H17	0.000335	$12.6140	3.81872	0.0133%
6	6	DAS	H17	0.004141	$12.6670	3.85703	0.1635%
6	6	DAS	S17	0.007887	$12.4990	3.81072	0.3155%
6	6	noDAS	S17	0.004453	$12.4480	3.77374	0.1789%
1	8	noDAS	H17	0.002451	$15.8170	4.86348	0.0775%
1	8	DAS	H17	0.006842	$15.9150	4.92350	0.2149%
1	8	DAS	S17	0.011572	$15.2810	4.76281	0.3786%

PLAYERS	DECKS	DAS	H17	WIN RATE	AVG. BET	SD	EXP.
1	8	noDAS	S17	0.007339	$15.1950	4.70755	0.2415%
6	8	noDAS	H17	-0.000252	$13.2350	4.20617	-0.0095%
6	8	DAS	H17	0.003120	$13.2780	4.24529	0.1175%
6	8	DAS	S17	0.007493	$13.0490	4.17924	0.2871%
6	8	noDAS	S17	0.004005	$13.0070	4.14132	0.1539%

To understand how to use these tables, let's look at an example.

Suppose you are playing a two-deck DAS/S17 blackjack game at a fairly full table, and your minimum bet size is $25.

Looking down the table at the 15th row, we see the matching game with six players. Going across, we see that the win rate is 0.009420 bet units per round. Let's suppose that we will play 60 rounds an hour (100 is too high, because there are lot of players at the table). Then our hourly win rate will be: 60 x 0.009420 x $25 = $14.13/hour. Our edge is 0.4614 percent, which tells us, on average, what we can expect to earn off every bet.

Earlier in the book we often quoted an hourly win rate for a $10 player of about $7.50 an hour. We can derive that figure from these tables as follows: the win rate for the two-deck game, DAS/H17, heads-up play is 0.007856, times 100 hands an hour, times $10 for the bet size, equals $7.86 per hour. For a six-deck DAS/S17 game, assuming a full table of six players, we get a win rate from the table of 0.007887, which is an hourly win rate of $7.89, assuming 100 hands per hour for a $10 bettor.

Please Note: *All games have a positive player edge, except for the one absolutely worst game (eight players, noDAS, H17).*

Excluding single-deck games, I simply move on to the next casino if I can't get DAS and S17, unless there is unusually good penetration or some other advantageous rule such as surrender. My favorite game is the two-deck/DAS/S17/67 percent penetration, which delivers an approximately healthy 0.5 percent edge, with the equivalent six-deck game close behind. And this is using the very low bet spread of Speed Count Conservative.

Very Aggressive Speed Count Performances

PLAYERS	DECKS	DAS	H17	WIN RATE	AVG. BET	SD	EXP.
1	1	noDAS	H17	0.024598	$12.4140	3.17941	0.9908%
1	1	DAS	H17	0.027756	$12.4850	3.20652	1.1116%
1	1	DAS	S17	0.031100	$12.3670	3.17071	1.2574%
1	1	noDAS	S17	0.028084	$12.2740	3.14361	1.1441%
6	1	noDAS	H17	0.035334	$12.5480	3.29473	1.3739%
6	1	DAS	H17	0.038344	$12.6000	3.31701	1.4877%
6	1	DAS	S17	0.041232	$12.5490	3.29557	1.6243%
6	1	noDAS	S17	0.038154	$12.4180	3.26171	1.5178%
1	2	noDAS	H17	0.019322	$14.3800	3.72191	0.6718%
1	2	DAS	H17	0.023314	$14.4710	3.75972	0.8056%
1	2	DAS	S17	0.026905	$14.2500	3.70103	0.9440%
1	2	noDAS	S17	0.023101	$14.1680	3.66581	0.8152%
6	2	noDAS	H17	0.022732	$14.1020	3.74732	0.8060%
6	2	DAS	H17	0.026423	$14.1680	3.77937	0.9325%
6	2	DAS	S17	0.030455	$14.0680	3.74746	1.0824%
6	2	noDAS	S17	0.026827	$14.0070	3.71680	0.9576%
1	4	noDAS	H17	0.020224	$20.5060	6.03466	0.4931%
1	4	DAS	H17	0.025895	$20.6240	6.09862	0.6278%
1	4	DAS	S17	0.031175	$20.0090	5.94473	0.7790%
1	4	noDAS	S17	0.025932	$19.9050	5.88520	0.6514%
6	4	noDAS	H17	0.024033	$19.8470	5.99180	0.6054%
6	4	DAS	H17	0.029278	$19.9070	6.04342	0.7354%
6	4	DAS	S17	0.034498	$19.6290	5.96354	0.8788%
6	4	noDAS	S17	0.029679	$19.5760	5.91496	0.7580%
1	6	noDAS	H17	0.019863	$22.2000	7.65193	0.4474%
1	6	DAS	H17	0.025895	$22.3000	7.72957	0.5806%
1	6	DAS	S17	0.031774	$21.3560	7.46807	0.7439%
1	6	noDAS	S17	0.025966	$21.2710	7.39683	0.6104%
6	6	noDAS	H17	0.020576	$20.9820	7.43837	0.4903%
6	6	DAS	H17	0.026020	$21.0010	7.49397	0.6195%
6	6	DAS	S17	0.032010	$20.5880	7.36594	0.7774%
6	6	noDAS	S17	0.026544	$20.5710	7.31279	0.6452%
1	8	noDAS	H17	0.013704	$23.8000	8.15145	0.2879%
1	8	DAS	H17	0.020203	$23.9010	8.23618	0.4226%
1	8	DAS	S17	0.026395	$22.7420	7.92802	0.5803%

PLAYERS	DECKS	DAS	H17	WIN RATE	AVG. BET	SD	EXP.
1	8	noDAS	S17	0.020102	$22.6550	7.85007	0.4436%
6	8	noDAS	H17	0.015621	$22.1640	7.83288	0.3524%
6	8	DAS	H17	0.021322	$22.1680	7.89139	0.4809%
6	8	DAS	S17	0.027389	$21.6650	7.74281	0.6321%
6	8	noDAS	S17	0.021815	$21.6610	7.68652	0.5036%

The Very Aggressive Speed Count improves your earnings substantially by increasing the bets you make when you have a positive edge over the casino. For example, our win rate in the two-deck/DAS/S17/one-player game was 0.011103 units with Speed Count Conservative but is 0.026905 with Very Aggressive. If you are a $10 player, then that's a difference in hourly win rate of $11 for the Speed Count Conservative as compared to $26.90 with Speed Count Very Aggressive in this specific game (2.5 times better, assuming 100 rounds per hour).

Of course, this extra performance comes with increased risk and bankroll requirements. Following the tables in Chapter 8, we can see that Speed Count Very Aggressive calls for a bet spread of one to 15 units in a two-deck game (top bet of three hands of five units at a Speed Count of 36). This is definitely *very aggressive* and exactly the kind of action that will get the pit bosses scrutinizing your play.

All the same, I personally will use an even higher bet spread for very short hit-and-run sessions at casinos with very good double-deck penetration. After an exceptionally big win after multiple high bets, I check my watch and suddenly discover that it's time to catch up with friends...then to the cage and homeward bound! Playing advantage blackjack with a 1 percent edge or more is fun, but like most high-risk sports, it is best to do in small bursts. And of course, I always play with a substantial session bankroll at all times. I cringe and caution students when, ripe with the excitement of learning card counting, they declare they're off to beat the casinos with a couple hundred bucks in their pockets. Bad idea.

Aggressive Speed Count Performance

PLAYERS	DECKS	DAS	H17	WIN RATE	AVG. BET	SD	EXP.
1	1	noDAS	H17	0.012403	$9.0560	2.11986	0.6848%
1	1	DAS	H17	0.014753	$9.1170	2.14113	0.8091%
1	1	DAS	S17	0.017232	$9.0590	2.12604	0.9511%
1	1	noDAS	S17	0.014916	$8.9900	2.10332	0.8296%
6	1	noDAS	H17	0.010321	$8.1390	1.92296	0.6340%
6	1	DAS	H17	0.012429	$8.1910	1.94161	0.7586%
6	1	DAS	S17	0.014852	$8.1690	1.93450	0.9091%
6	1	noDAS	S17	0.012664	$8.0910	1.91001	0.7825%
1	2	noDAS	H17	0.011364	$11.9310	2.88853	0.4762%
1	2	DAS	H17	0.014614	$12.0180	2.92254	0.6080%
1	2	DAS	S17	0.017955	$11.8870	2.89176	0.7552%
1	2	noDAS	S17	0.014863	$11.8080	2.85979	0.6294%
6	2	noDAS	H17	0.009394	$10.7410	2.65636	0.4373%
6	2	DAS	H17	0.012368	$10.8160	2.68642	0.5718%
6	2	DAS	S17	0.015685	$10.7620	2.67190	0.7287%
6	2	noDAS	S17	0.012763	$10.6930	2.64324	0.5968%
1	4	noDAS	H17	0.011563	$16.7280	4.59585	0.3456%
1	4	DAS	H17	0.016330	$16.8460	4.65328	0.4847%
1	4	DAS	S17	0.020943	$16.4590	4.56665	0.6362%
1	4	noDAS	S17	0.016397	$16.3540	4.51322	0.5013%
6	4	noDAS	H17	0.009505	$14.7200	4.16927	0.3228%
6	4	DAS	H17	0.013453	$14.7890	4.21323	0.4548%
6	4	DAS	S17	0.018164	$14.6490	4.17752	0.6200%
6	4	noDAS	S17	0.014333	$14.5850	4.13570	0.4914%
1	6	noDAS	H17	0.012387	$17.8210	5.63668	0.3475%
1	6	DAS	H17	0.017102	$17.9280	5.70345	0.4770%
1	6	DAS	S17	0.022002	$17.3000	5.54402	0.6359%
1	6	noDAS	S17	0.017437	$17.2080	5.48317	0.5067%
6	6	noDAS	H17	0.007258	$15.2130	4.98587	0.2385%
6	6	DAS	H17	0.011921	$15.2580	5.03166	0.3906%
6	6	DAS	S17	0.016298	$15.0330	4.96673	0.5421%
6	6	noDAS	S17	0.012252	$14.9900	4.92273	0.4087%
1	8	noDAS	H17	0.007545	$18.6920	5.92329	0.2018%
1	8	DAS	H17	0.012800	$18.8020	5.99636	0.3404%
1	8	DAS	S17	0.018430	$18.0490	5.81062	0.5105%

PLAYERS	DECKS	DAS	H17	WIN RATE	AVG. BET	SD	EXP.
1	8	noDAS	S17	0.013387	$17.9540	5.74334	0.3728%
6	8	noDAS	H17	0.004892	$15.6940	5.18665	0.1559%
6	8	DAS	H17	0.008833	$15.7380	5.23565	0.2806%
6	8	DAS	S17	0.013982	$15.4660	5.15936	0.4520%
6	8	noDAS	S17	0.009719	$15.4240	5.11201	0.3151%

This strategy is an attempt to sit in between the extremes of Conservative and the Very Aggressive Speed Count. But the reality is that all players should experiment with their own variations of Speed Count betting to discover what method delivers the performance they want, with acceptable bankroll risk, and the least attraction of casino heat.

There is no right way to bet or play, as long as you are betting more than your unit bet size above counts of 30 and as little as possible below 31. There is sometimes a lot of discussion about optimal bet spreads, which I still find very strange outside of the ivory towers of blackjack academia. The optimal bet spread is zero below the bet pivot (31 for Speed Count), and the maximum allowed table bet above it! Of course, pragmatics and real bankrolls constrain this approach. Although it is true that betting a rational spread of 1/2/4/6/8 will obviously perform better than 1/1/1/8, the reality is that what you bet above the pivot should be what you can afford and what you can get away with in the casino. Applying the *Kelly Criterion*—which is betting a percentage of your total bankroll based on percentage of edge—is nice in principle but impractical in today's casinos that scrutinize every big bet and unusual play.

The only difference from Speed Count Aggressive and Very Aggressive is the absence of hand-spreading. We use the slightly higher bet spread, exit on rotten counts, and insure at high counts. This lowers our risk and bankroll requirement substantially, while still delivering improved win rates. The double-deck/DAS/S17/1-player game we examined earlier here has a win rate of 0.017955, which works out to about $18 per hour win rate for the $10 player (Conservative Speed Count yielded $11, while Very Aggressive was $26.90).

As you mix and match to come up with your own Speed Count strategy, just remember to increase your bet above the pivot in some gradual spread, do not play hands (or just leave the shoe) when the count dives below the starting count, and press those bets when the count skyrockets in the high 30s or 40s. Play with the right bankroll for your game to maintain no more than five percent Risk of Ruin, and you will be on the way to winning at blackjack.

Bankroll: Conservative Speed Count

PLAYERS	DECKS	DAS	H17	LROR	TRIP: 400	TRIP: 1200	TRIP: 4000
1	1	noDAS	H17	$4,826	$363	$618	$1,084
1	1	DAS	H17	$3,572	$364	$614	$1,064
1	1	DAS	S17	$2,682	$358	$597	$1,016
1	1	noDAS	S17	$3,339	$357	$600	$1,037
6	1	noDAS	H17	$4,701	$331	$563	$992
6	1	DAS	H17	$3,417	$331	$559	$971
6	1	DAS	S17	$2,514	$326	$545	$933
6	1	noDAS	S17	$3,171	$325	$548	$948
1	2	noDAS	H17	$11,951	$531	$908	$1,622
1	2	DAS	H17	$7,361	$532	$906	$1,596
1	2	DAS	S17	$5,111	$522	$879	$1,527
1	2	noDAS	S17	$6,809	$519	$885	$1,549
6	2	noDAS	H17	$13,522	$486	$832	$1,492
6	2	DAS	H17	$7,766	$488	$831	$1,472
6	2	DAS	S17	$5,068	$480	$812	$1,411
6	2	noDAS	S17	$6,961	$478	$813	$1,435
1	4	noDAS	H17	$36,202	$590	$1,017	$1,847
1	4	DAS	H17	$13,443	$591	$1,014	$1,812
1	4	DAS	S17	$7,796	$575	$979	$1,721
1	4	noDAS	S17	$12,081	$575	$982	$1,752
6	4	noDAS	H17	$73,793	$541	$933	$1,694
6	4	DAS	H17	$16,037	$541	$928	$1,668
6	4	DAS	S17	$7,897	$530	$903	$1,597
6	4	noDAS	S17	$12,621	$530	$906	$1,621
1	6	noDAS	H17	$33,976	$838	$1,444	$2,605
1	6	DAS	H17	$17,944	$841	$1,442	$2,576
1	6	DAS	S17	$11,265	$814	$1,381	$2,432
1	6	noDAS	S17	$15,986	$808	$1,382	$2,467
6	6	noDAS	H17	$326,394	$747	$1,295	$2,361

PLAYERS	DECKS	DAS	H17	LROR	TRIP: 400	TRIP: 1200	TRIP: 4000
6	6	DAS	H17	$26,906	$749	$1,288	$2,326
6	6	DAS	S17	$13,789	$734	$1,253	$2,236
6	6	noDAS	S17	$23,950	$731	$1,257	$2,269
1	8	noDAS	H17	$72,290	$949	$1,642	$2,974
1	8	DAS	H17	$26,535	$953	$1,639	$2,941
1	8	DAS	S17	$14,681	$914	$1,559	$2,760
1	8	noDAS	S17	$22,613	$911	$1,563	$2,794
6	8	noDAS	H17	N/A	N/A	N/A	N/A
6	8	DAS	H17	$43,261	$827	$1,426	$2,577
6	8	DAS	S17	$17,457	$806	$1,381	$2,464
6	8	noDAS	S17	$32,075	$807	$1,386	$2,498

If I could put a flashing light and a READ ME alert on these bankroll tables to make sure readers visit them, I would.

In all my experience teaching students card counting, the biggest mistake is not playing with enough money. I hope you've picked this up in the book by now and will come to these tables to find out exactly how much money you need to play with to not go broke (or at least, lower this probability). Or better yet, invest in software that includes the bankroll assessment and analysis tools, such as Blackjack Counter and Audit from my company.

LROR refers to Lifetime Risk of Ruin and means the amount of money you should set aside to play for your entire blackjack career and have no more than a 5 percent chance of losing it.

Trip ROR refers to the amount of money you should bring for a single outing or session of blackjack, such as a weekend trip or evening of playing. The required trip bankroll depends on how long you want to play. Presuming 100 hands per hour, the 1,200 column above might represent a typical weekend outing of 12 hours or 1,200 rounds of play, 400 an average evening session of four hours of play, and 4,000 per week of playing.

The tables assume the same game characteristics we've outlined before. Also, they are computing the 5 percent Risk of Ruin bankroll values (the bankroll required to have at most 5 percent chance of losing that money playing). More important, note that the dollar amounts above assume a $5 unit bet size.

So let's say your unit bet size (minimum bet size) is $25, and you're consistently playing that sweet double-deck/DAS/S17/one-player game. Looking at the 11th row, we can see that the "one night" 400 round-trip ROR is $522 for a $5 bettor. Hence, for a $25 bettor we should not go play that night with less than 5 x $522 = approximately a $2,6100 session bankroll to minimize the risk of going broke (he will have only a 5 percent chance of walking out broke as a $25 player).

Want to last over the long haul as a for-profit player? You better stash away $5,000 x 5 = $25,000 in a 401G right from the start. Only by doing so will you be able to manage the inevitable swings and occasional losing streaks that are bound to happen. These are sobering bankroll amounts for most new card counters.

Bankroll: Very Aggressive Speed Count

PLAYERS	DECKS	DAS	H17	LROR	TRIP: 400	TRIP: 1200	TRIP: 4000
1	1	noDAS	H17	$3,078	$583	$959	$1,575
1	1	DAS	H17	$2,774	$583	$954	$1,550
1	1	DAS	S17	$2,421	$570	$927	$1,476
1	1	noDAS	S17	$2,635	$569	$932	$1,503
6	1	noDAS	H17	$2,358	$590	$949	$1,502
6	1	DAS	H17	$2,198	$588	$945	$1,477
6	1	DAS	S17	$1,995	$579	$920	$1,411
6	1	noDAS	S17	$2,114	$578	$925	$1,437
1	2	noDAS	H17	$5,369	$698	$1,170	$1,993
1	2	DAS	H17	$4,541	$699	$1,162	$1,951
1	2	DAS	S17	$3,813	$682	$1,125	$1,862
1	2	noDAS	S17	$4,357	$681	$1,132	$1,898
6	2	noDAS	H17	$4,627	$696	$1,161	$1,952
6	2	DAS	H17	$4,049	$696	$1,155	$1,914
6	2	DAS	S17	$3,454	$685	$1,123	$1,835
6	2	noDAS	S17	$3,857	$686	$1,130	$1,876
1	4	noDAS	H17	$13,486	$1,149	$1,949	$3,411
1	4	DAS	H17	$10,757	$1,151	$1,944	$3,362
1	4	DAS	S17	$8,490	$1,111	$1,866	$3,184
1	4	noDAS	S17	$10,003	$1,109	$1,866	$3,224
6	4	noDAS	H17	$11,188	$1,137	$1,912	$3,322
6	4	DAS	H17	$9,343	$1,136	$1,907	$3,266

PLAYERS	DECKS	DAS	H17	LROR	TRIP: 400	TRIP: 1200	TRIP: 4000
6	4	DAS	S17	$7,721	$1,112	$1,855	$3,137
6	4	noDAS	S17	$8,829	$1,112	$1,863	$3,190
1	6	noDAS	H17	$22,077	$1,466	$2,501	$4,420
1	6	DAS	H17	$17,280	$1,473	$2,498	$4,371
1	6	DAS	S17	$13,146	$1,412	$2,375	$4,108
1	6	noDAS	S17	$15,781	$1,406	$2,381	$4,161
6	6	noDAS	H17	$20,139	$1,426	$2,419	$4,268
6	6	DAS	H17	$16,165	$1,425	$2,415	$4,215
6	6	DAS	S17	$12,695	$1,389	$2,343	$4,042
6	6	noDAS	S17	$15,088	$1,389	$2,350	$4,096
1	8	noDAS	H17	$36,313	$1,578	$2,695	$4,823
1	8	DAS	H17	$25,147	$1,584	$2,695	$4,764
1	8	DAS	S17	$17,834	$1,507	$2,560	$4,476
1	8	noDAS	S17	$22,959	$1,502	$2,567	$4,529
6	8	noDAS	H17	$29,416	$1,508	$2,586	$4,596
6	8	DAS	H17	$21,874	$1,512	$2,574	$4,529
6	8	DAS	S17	$16,393	$1,473	$2,498	$4,355
6	8	noDAS	S17	$20,283	$1,471	$2,496	$4,398

The Very Aggressive Speed Count bankroll tables are well worth examining in detail. Not surprisingly, you will find that you need a lot more money to play aggressively.

But let's take a closer look at the Lifetime Risk of Ruin for our favorite double-deck/DAS/S17 one-player game (row 11). We already saw that $522 was required for a typical evening playing session at $5 tables. Referring to the previous tables, we see that the equivalent bankroll for Speed Count Very Aggressive is $682, which is substantially higher, as expected. But the 5 percent lifetime Risk of Ruin bankroll is $3,813, which is substantially lower than the equivalent $5,111 bankroll for Speed Count Conservative! How can that be?

Risk of Ruin is a complex mathematical property, that depends on much more than just the standard deviation (or variance). It also factors in your win rate. Although Speed Count Very Aggressive clearly has a higher variance due to the increased bets, it also produces better earnings.

In the long run (Lifetime Risk of Ruin), the improved performance pays off and actually lowers our risk, while making us more money, clearly the best of both worlds—as long as we bring enough money to the tables every time we play and the casino doesn't give us the boot for our aggressive playing style.

I'm not including bankroll tables for Speed Count Aggressive (our "middle-of-the-road" strategy), because I've already noted that it's a matter of personal taste and comfort to tune Speed Count the way you like it.

During the course of developing Speed Count, I generated a ton of additional simulation data that is not provided in this book. But I hope you get the point—namely, that Speed Count is not only easy to learn and use but it has the power to give you the edge over the casino when you play blackjack.

Now, that's exciting!

CHAPTER 19

Spanish 21

A popular variation of blackjack called *Spanish 21* has entered the casino fray. With the proper Spanish 21 Basic Strategy, the house edge can hover between 0.40 percent and 0.76 percent. That translates into long-term losses between 40 cents and 76 cents per $100 wagered. In short, played properly, Spanish 21 is a good game.

The following strategies were created by Michael Shackleford, also known as "the Wizard of Odds." Michael is a professional actuary and an expert in the math of casino games. He was an adjunct professor of casino math at the University of Nevada. He is the author of the book *Gambling 102*, published by Huntington Press. Michael's website is www. wizardofodds.com.

The Rules

Spanish 21 uses six or eight decks, each deck consisting of only 48 cards— the four 10s have been removed. To make up for the limited number of 10-valued cards, Spanish 21 gives to the player a host of bonuses and favorable rules. The rules are based on liberal six- or eight-deck blackjack rules, including double after split, late surrender, and resplitting aces. In addition, Spanish 21 offers the following rule enhancements:

- A player 21 always wins.
- A player's blackjack beats a dealer's blackjack.
- A player may double on any number of cards.
- At some casinos, a player may usually hit and double down after splitting aces.

- Players may surrender after doubling, known as "double down rescue." The player forfeits an amount equal to his original bet.
- A five-card 21 pays 3-to-2, a six-card 21 pays 2-to-1, a seven-or-more-card 21 pays 3-to-1. However, the bonuses are not paid if the player doubled.
- A 6-7-8 or 7-7-7 of mixed suits pays 3-to-2, of the same suit pays 2-to-1, and of spades pays 3-to-1. These bonuses do not pay after doubling.
- Suited 7-7-7 when the dealer has a 7 face up pays $1,000 for bets of $5 to $24 and $5,000 for bets of $25 or over. In addition, all other players receive a $50 "envy bonus." This bonus does not pay after doubling or splitting.

Variable Rules
- Dealer may hit or stand on a Soft 17.
- Usually six or eight Spanish decks are used.
- Some casinos allow redoubling up to three times.
- Some casinos allow late surrender on the initial two cards.

Basic Strategy for Spanish 21
Dealer HITS Soft 17

S = Stand	H = Hit	P = Split
S4 = Stand except hit with four or more cards	D = Double	PS = Split except hit with suited 7s
S5 = Stand except hit with five or more cards	D3 = Double except hit with three or more cards	@ = Hit if suited or spaded 6-7-8 is possible
S6 = Stand except hit with six or more cards	D4 = Double except hit with four or more cards	*Hit if any 6-7-8 is possible
R = Surrender	D5 = Double except hit with five or more cards	**Hit if spaded 6-7-8 is possible
R/H = Surrender, if allowed		

Hand	2	3	4	5	6	7	8	9	10	Ace
4-8	H	H	H	H	H	H	H	H	H	H
9	H	H	H	H	D	H	H	H	H	H
10	D5	D5	D	D	D	D4	D3	H	H	H

Hand	2	3	4	5	6	7	8	9	10	Ace
11	D4	D5	D5	D5	D5	D4	D4	D4	D3	D3
12	H	H	H	H	H	H	H	H	H	H
13	H	H	H	H	S4*	H	H	H	H	H
14	H	H	S4*	S5@	S6**	H	H	H	H	H
15	S4*	S5@	S6	S6	S	H	H	H	H	H
16	S6	S6	S6	S	S	H	H	H	H	R/H
17	S	S	S	S	S	S	S6	S6	S6	R/H
18-21	S	S	S	S	S	S	S	S	S	S
Soft 12	H	H	H	H	H	H	H	H	H	H
Soft 13	H	H	H	H	H	H	H	H	H	H
Soft 14	H	H	H	H	H	H	H	H	H	H
Soft 15	H	H	H	H	D4	H	H	H	H	H
Soft 16	H	H	H	D3	D4	H	H	H	H	H
Soft 17	H	H	D3	D4	D5	H	H	H	H	H
Soft 18	S4	S4	D4	D5	D6	S6	S4	H	H	H
Soft 19	S	S	S	S	S	S	S	S	S6	S6
2-2	P	P	P	P	P	P	P	H	H	H
3-3	P	P	P	P	P	P	P	H	H	H
4-4	H	H	H	H	H	H	H	H	H	H
5-5	D5	D5	D	D	D	D4	D3	H	H	H
6-6	H	H	P	P	P	H	H	H	H	H
7-7	P	P	P	P	P	PS	H	H	H	H
8-8	P	P	P	P	P	P	P	P	P	R
9-9	S	P	P	P	P	S	P	P	S	S
10-10	S	S	S	S	S	S	S	S	S	S
A-A	P	P	P	P	P	P	P	P	P	P

Basic Strategy for Spanish 21
Dealer STANDS Soft 17

S = Stand	H = Hit	P = Split
S4 = Stand except hit with four or more cards	D = Double	PS = Split except hit with suited 7s
S5 = Stand except hit with five or more cards	D3 = Double except hit with three or more cards	@ = Hit if suited or spaded 6-7-8 is possible
S6 = Stand except hit with six or more cards	D4 = Double except hit with four or more cards	*Hit if any 6-7-8 is possible
R = Surrender	D5 = Double except hit with five or more cards	**Hit if spaded 6-7-8 is possible
R/H = Surrender, if allowed		

Hand	2	3	4	5	6	7	8	9	10	Ace
4-8	H	H	H	H	H	H	H	H	H	H
9	H	H	H	H	D4	H	H	H	H	H
10	D5	D5	D	D	D	D4	D3	H	H	H
11	D4	D5	D5	D5	D5	D4	D4	D4	D3	D3
12	H	H	H	H	H	H	H	H	H	H
13	H	H	H	H	H	H	H	H	H	H
14	H	H	S4*	S5*	S4*	H	H	H	H	H
15	S4*	S5*	S5**	S6	S6	H	H	H	H	H
16	S5	S6	S6	S	S	H	H	H	H	H
17	S	S	S	S	S	S	S6	S6	S6	R/H
18 to 21	S	S	S	S	S	S	S	S	S	S
Soft 12 to 15	H	H	H	H	H	H	H	H	H	H
Soft 16	H	H	H	H	D4	H	H	H	H	H
Soft 17	H	H	D3	D4	D5	H	H	H	H	H
Soft 18	S4	S4	D4	D5	D5	S6	S4	H	H	H

Hand	2	3	4	5	6	7	8	9	10	Ace
Soft 19 to 21	S	S	S	S	S	S	S	S	S6	S
2-2	P	P	P	P	P	P	P	H	H	H
3-3	P	P	P	P	P	P	P	H	H	H
4-4	H	H	H	H	H	H	H	H	H	H
5-5	D5	D5	D	D	D	D4	D3	H	H	H
6-6	H	H	P	P	P	H	H	H	H	H
7-7	P	P	P	P	P	PS	H	H	H	H
8-8	P	P	P	P	P	P	P	P	P	P
9-9	S	P	P	P	P	S	P	P	S	S
10-10	S	S	S	S	S	S	S	S	S	S
A-A	P	P	P	P	P	P	P	P	P	P

Please Note: *If drawing to split aces is not allowed and the dealer stands on Soft 17, then hit A-A against an ace.*

Basic Strategy for Spanish 21
Double Double Down/Dealer Hits Soft 17
Player Has Not Already Doubled

S = Stand		H = Hit		P = Split	
S4 = Stand except hit with four or more cards		D = Double		PS = Split except hit with suited 7s	
S5 = Stand except hit with five or more cards		D3 = Double except hit with three or more cards		@ = Hit if suited or spaded 6-7-8 is possible	
S6 = Stand except hit with six or more cards		D4 = Double except hit with four or more cards		*Hit if any 6-7-8 is possible	
R = Surrender		D5 = Double except hit with five or more cards		**Hit if spaded 6-7-8 is possible	
R/H = Surrender, if allowed			$ Hit with Super Bonus		

Hand	2	3	4	5	6	7	8	9	10	Ace
5	H	H	H	H	D	H	H	H	H	H
6	H	H	H	H	D	H	H	H	H	H
7	H	H	H	H	D	H	H	H	H	H
8	H	H	H	D	D	H	H	H	H	H
9	H	D4	D	D	D	H	H	H	H	H
10	D5	D5	D	D	D	D	D5	H	H	H
11	D4	D5	D5	D5	D5	D5	D5	D4	D3	D3
12	H	H	H	H	H	H	H	H	H	H
13	H	H	H	H	S4*	H	H	H	H	H
14	H	H	S4*	S5@	S6**	H	H	H	H	H
15	S4*	S5@	S6	S6	S	H	H	H	H	H
16	S6	S6	S6	S	S	H	H	H	H	R/H
17	S	S	S	S	S	S	S6	S6	S6	R/H
18 to 21	S	S	S	S	S	S	S	S	S	S
A2	H	D3	D	D	D	H	H	H	H	H
A3	H	D3	D4	D	D	H	H	H	H	H
A4	H	H	D4	D4	D5	H	H	H	H	H
A5	H	H	D3	D4	D5	H	H	H	H	H
A6	H	H	D3	D4	D5	H	H	H	H	H
A7	S4	S4	D4	D5	D6	S6	S4	H	H	H

Hand	2	3	4	5	6	7	8	9	10	Ace
A8	S	S	S	S	S	S	S	S	S6	S6
2-2	P	P	P	P	P	P	P	H	H	H
3-3	P	P	P	P	P	P	P	H	H	H
4-4	H	H	H	H	H	H	H	H	H	H
5-5	D5	D5	D	D	D	D	D5	H	H	H
6-6	H	H	P	P	P	H	H	H	H	H
7-7	P	P	P	P	P	PS	H	H	H	H
8-8	P	P	P	P	P	P	P	P	P	R
9-9	S	P	P	P	P	S	P	P	S	S
10-10	S	S	S	S	S	S	S	S	S	S
A-A	P	P	P	P	P	P	P	P	P	P

Double Down Surrender: 12-16 against 8-Ace; 17 against an Ace. Never split 4s, 5s, or 10s.

Basic Strategy for Spanish 21
Double Double Down, Dealer Hits Soft 17
Player Has Already Doubled

S = Stand			R = Surrender			D = Double			

	2	3	4	5	6	7	8	9	10	Ace
6	S	D	D	D	D	D	R	R	R	R
7	D	D	D	D	D	D	R	R	R	R
8	D	D	D	D	D	D	D	D	R	R
9	D	D	D	D	D	D	D	D	D	D
10	D	D	D	D	D	D	D	D	D	D
11	D	D	D	D	D	D	D	D	D	D
12	S	S	S	S	S	D	D	R	R	R
13	S	S	S	S	S	S	R	R	R	R
14	S	S	S	S	S	S	R	R	R	R
15	S	S	S	S	S	S	R	R	R	R
16	S	S	S	S	S	S	R	R	R	R
17	S	S	S	S	S	S	S	S	S	R

	2	3	4	5	6	7	8	9	10	Ace
18-21	S	S	S	S	S	S	S	S	S	S
Soft 13	D	D	D	D	D	D	D	D	D	D
Soft 14	D	D	D	D	D	D	D	D	D	D
Soft 15	D	D	D	D	D	D	D	D	D	D
Soft 16	D	D	D	D	D	D	D	D	D	D
Soft 17	D	D	D	D	D	D	D	D	D	D
Soft 18	S	S	D	D	D	S	S	S	S	S
Soft 19	S	S	S	S	S	S	S	S	S	S
Soft 20	S	S	S	S	S	S	S	S	S	S
Soft 21	S	S	S	S	S	S	S	S	S	S

Please Note: *Many readers have expressed doubt about Shackleford's advice to hit 17 against an ace with three or more cards. The player will save about 2.8 percent of the initial wager by hitting as opposed to standing. The dealers will advise against this play, as might other players, but the odds favor hitting.*

House Edges

Following are the house edges under various common rules, before considering the Super Bonus.

- Dealer stands on Soft 17 = 0.40 percent
- Dealer hits on Soft 17 and redoubling allowed = 0.42 percent
- Dealer hits on Soft 17 and redoubling not allowed = 0.76 percent

Super Bonus

The probability of hitting the Super Bonus is one in 668,382 with six decks and one in 549,188 with eight decks. The reduction in the house edge depends on the bet amount, and to a lesser extent, the number of players. With no other players and bets of exactly $5 or $25, the Super Bonus lowers the house edge by 0.030 percent in a six-deck game and by 0.036 percent in an eight-deck game.

At a bet of exactly $5, the envy bonus lowers the house edge by an additional 0.0015 percent in a six-deck game and by 0.0018 percent in an eight-deck game, per additional player.

For bet amounts other than those indicated here, the benefit of the Super Bonus will go down as the bet amount goes up.

Rule Variations

- **No draw to split aces:** This rule increases the house edge by 0.29 percent (29 cents per $100 wagered). Therefore, hit A:A against an ace if drawing to split aces is not allowed and the dealer stands on Soft 17.
- **Ace and 10 after splitting aces pays 3-to-2:** This lowers the house edge by 0.16 percent (16 cents per $100 wagered).
- **Doubling allowed only on first two cards:** This would increase the house edge by 0.16 percent.
- **Match the dealer:** In some locations there is a side bet available if the either or both of the player's first two cards match the dealer's up-card. In a six-deck game, a non-suited match pays 4-to-1 and a suited match pays 9-to-1. In an eight-deck game a non-suited match pays 3-to-1 and a suited match pays 12-to-1. The six-deck game side bet has a house edge of 3.06 percent; with eight decks it is 2.99 percent—edges that are way too high to bother with.

CHAPTER 20
For Bad Boys and Girls

A Simplified Basic Strategy

The Wizard of Odds has developed a simplified Basic Strategy that is easy to memorize for those players who just don't wish to learn the stronger traditional Basic Strategies in this book or for those who do not want to bring a card to the table to play perfectly. In excellent blackjack games, the cost of using this strategy is usually less than two-tenths of a percent over the perfect Basic Strategy. Not bad if you are a bad boy or girl who doesn't want to play the strongest method against the casinos, which is Speed Count and the OBS.

Hand	2 through 6	7 through Ace
4 to 8	Hit	Hit
9	Double	Hit
10 or 11	Double	Double when your hand is higher than dealer's up-card
12 to 16	Stand	Hit
17 to 21	Stand	Stand
Ace-2 through Ace-4	Hit	Hit
Ace-5 through Ace-7	Double	Hit
Ace-8 through Ace-10	Stand	Stand
2:2; 3:3; 6:6; 7:7; 9:9	Split	Do Not Split
4:4; 5:5; 10:10	Do Not Split	Do Not Split
8:8; A:A	Split	Split

In addition:

- Surrender 16 against a 10, if allowed.
- Never take insurance.
- If not allowed to double, then hit the hand, except stand on A:7.
- If the strategy says to double, but you have three or more cards or table rules don't allow soft doubling, then hit; except, stand with a Soft 18.
- If the strategy says "do not split," then treat the hand as a hard total of 8, 10, or 20, according to the pair in question.

Glossary

Ace: An ace can count as either 1 or 11. It is always assumed that an ace in your hand counts as 11 unless your hand exceeds 21, in which case the ace reverts to a value of one.

Action: The total amount of money that a player wagers over a period of time.

Advantage Player: A player who has the mathematical advantage over the casino.

Anchor Player: The player seated in third base and the last to act before the dealer acts on his hand.

Automatic Shuffling Machine: A machine used to preshuffle a separate shoe of cards, so that it is ready to be used after the current shoe is exhausted. Compare to Continuous Shuffling Machine.

Average Bet: The average of the total amount of a player's wagers per round.

Back Counting: Playing technique in which a player stands behind a table and counts the cards as a spectator with the intent of entering the game when the count becomes player favorable.

Backed Off: If a casino supervisor, while you are playing blackjack, asks you to stop playing. Generally when you are backed off, you are not read the trespass act or barred.

Bankroll: The money you use to gamble.

Barring: When a casino supervisor tells you that you are permanently prohibited from playing blackjack in the casino.

Basic Strategy: The mathematically optimum way to play your hand based solely on the player's first two cards and the dealer's up-card. Good Basic Strategy minimizes the casino's edge over the player.

Bet Sizing: Scaling the size of your bet in relation to your mathematical advantage over the casino.

Bet Spread: The range between a player's minimum and maximum bets.

Betting Spot: Also called the betting circle or square, it's the designated area on the layout in front of a player where the player places his bet.

Bet Unit: Refers to the amount of your unit (usually minimum) bet size. Most blackjack math is done in bet units to generalize the results for all players.

Blackjack: When the player's initial two cards consists of an ace and a 10-value card. Also called a "21."

Blackjack Counter: A player who monitors the dealt cards in some fashion that indicates who has an advantage (the casino or player) and by how much. Counters can use one of many different count systems, which all come down to measuring the disproportionate distribution of remaining cards. Depending on the count and the advantage it indicates, the player will bet more or less money.

Blacks: Black-colored casino chips worth $100 in denomination.

Black-Chip Player: A player who wagers $100 or more per hand.

Burn Card: After the dealer shuffles the cards and they are cut, it's the top card, which is removed from play.

Bust: When a player's hand totals more than 21.

Buy-In: The exchange of a player's cash for casino chips.

Cage: The cashier area.

Camouflage: Techniques to disguise the fact that you are card counting.

Card Counter: A player who keeps track of specific cards as they are played for the purpose of knowing when the odds shift in his favor.

Casino Hold: For table games, the hold is a percentage of all the player's buy-in that is won by the casino.

Cheques: Fancy name for chips.

Chip Counting: The ability to count the value of the chips of your fellow players, usually done in a tournament.

Comp: A free product or service that the casino extends to its loyal players.

Continuous-Shuffling Machine (CSM): A shuffling machine that randomly mixes the discards from each round with the undealt cards. Card counting does not work against a CSM. Compare to Automatic Shuffling Machine.

Correlate: Betting the same as your opponent in a tournament.

Count: The value of the Speed Count. Also used to refer to the value of the counting metric with any count system.

Countdown: At certain times in a tournament the casino will count down all the players' chips so everyone knows what everyone has.

Cut Card: A colored plastic card inserted by the player into the shuffled decks of cards to determine where the dealer will cut the decks. When the cut card appears during a round, the round is completed, and then the decks are shuffled.

Cutoff: The unplayed cards remaining in the shoe after the cut card appears.

DAS: Double after pair splitting. NoDAS means that doubling after splitting is not allowed. DAS is an advantageous rule for the player.

Discards: The cards that are removed from a round of play and placed in the discard tray.

Discard Tray: A clear plastic device that holds the dealt cards during play.

Double Down: After a player receives his initial two cards, he has the option to make one secondary bet up to the amount of the initial bet and receive exactly one extra dealt card. The money for doubles can equal or be less than the original bet.

Down Card: Dealer's hole card or any card that is dealt face down.

Early Surrender: A player is allowed to surrender his hand before the dealer checks for a blackjack (see *Surrender*).

Edge: Generally refers to the mathematical advantage as a percentage the casino has over the player or vice versa. The edge is the average amount of each and every bet you make that you should expect to win or lose in the long run.

Emotional Bankroll: An amount of bankroll that allows a player to take naturally occurring and expected losses in stride.

Even Money: When the player has a blackjack hand and the dealer has an ace showing, the player has the option to take an even-money payoff before the dealer checks his hole card for a blackjack. Taking even money is the same as insuring the hand.

Exit Strategy: Leaving a blackjack table or not playing rounds when the count is very poor, indicating a high house edge.

Expectation: What the player can expect to win or lose over time, betting the way he bets.

Eye in the Sky: Usually refers to the cameras that are recording everything in the casinos.

401G: A money-market account with funds set aside only for gambling.

Face-Down Game: The players' initial two cards are dealt face down, and the players must handle the cards themselves.

Face-Up Game: The players' initial two cards are dealt face up, and the players are not permitted to handle or touch the cards.

Fat Finger Technique: Advantage-play method that can be used in a single- or double-deck game where the cards are dealt face up.

First Base: The player's seat located on the far right of the blackjack table that is dealt first (dealer's left side).

Floorman or Floor Person: Casino executive located in the pit and responsible for supervising a group of casino games.

Going for the Low: In tournament play, betting a small amount.

Greens: Chips in a casino valued at $25.

Grifter's Gambit: Inverse hand-spreading.

H17: Dealer must hit Soft 17. S17 where dealer stands on Soft 17 is a favorable and preferable rule for the player.

Hand-Spreading: Increasing the number of hands one plays if the count has gone positive.

Hard Hand: A hard hand is any hand that either does not contain an ace, or if it does, the ace must count as 1.

Heads Up: Playing alone with the dealer.

Heat: When casino executives scrutinize a player very carefully while he plays.

Hi-Lo: Traditional card-counting method.

Histogram: A chart using consecutive bars to represent a series of values across a category.

Hit: When a player requests another card or, by the rules, a dealer must draw another card.

Hole Card: The dealer's card that is dealt face down; also known as the down card.

Host: A casino employee who caters to casino players who wager a significant amount in the casino.

Insurance: Insurance is a side bet in which players are betting that the dealer's hole card will be a 10-value card. Players can make an insurance bet up to one half of the initial bet made on the hand. You win your insurance bet if the dealer has a 10-value card in the hole. A winning insurance bet pays off at 2-to-1 odds. *See also* Even Money.

Inverse Hand-Spreading: Betting on multiple hands and then going to one big hand when the count goes positive.

ISC: Initial Speed Count, or the value of the Speed Count at the start of a new shoe.

Kelly Criterion: Betting a percentage of your total bankroll based on the percent of your edge at any given time in a game.

Leader Board: In tournaments, a scoreboard that tells where all players stand versus all other players.

Live-Money Tournaments: Players must buy in and use their own money for a tournament, not just an entrance fee.

Lifetime Risk of Ruin (LROR): The amount of money a player should set aside to play for agreement entire blackjack career with no more than a fixed chance of losing it (typically chosen to be 5 percent).

Marker: A promissory note that can be drawn against your bank account.

Mid-Shoe Entry: A big question is what happens if you place a bet on the felt in the middle of a shoe? Some casinos will not allow you to make a bet if you have not been betting since the start of the shoe. This restriction is designed to hamper card counters from only betting when the count is favorable.

Money Plays: Playing with actual currency instead of chips.

Natural: Another name for a blackjack hand. Also called "21."

Negative Count: A count that favors the casinos.

Nickels: $5 denomination chips.

No Hole Card: In some games the dealer waits until the players have played their hands before giving himself a hole card.

Optimum Basic Strategy (OBS): A hand-playing strategy that is used by a player who uses Speed Count.

Pair Split: Splitting your pairs to make two hands. You must bet the same amount on the second hand as you did on the first.

Peek: When the dealer is dealt an ace or 10 up-card and manually checks the hole card to determine if he has a blackjack. Insurance is offered prior to the peek if the up-card is an ace. If the hand is a black-jack, the dealer flips the hand, and the round is done.

Penetration: The percentage of cards that are dealt before the shuffle.

Pivot Point: The value of the Speed Count where the player's expectation turns from negative to positive.

Pitch: A method used by the dealer to deal the cards to players usually in single- and double-deck games.

Pit: The area in the middle of a grouping of blackjack tables. Casino supervisors who monitor the games are located in the pit.

Pit Boss: Casino executive responsible for table games.

Play Variation: A deviation from the basic playing strategy used by advanced card counters based upon the count.

Ploppy: Slang term for an unskilled casino player.

Pontoon: Early form of blackjack.

Positive Count: A count that favors the players. In Speed Count, that would be 31 or higher.

Progressive Betting Systems: A method used by players to vary the size of their bets based upon the win/loss result of the previous hand. A betting system, without using card counting, is a good way to lose money (betting systems alone cannot help you win).

Push: When a player's hand totals the same as the dealer's hand (also known as a tie).

Pushing the House: Getting a better game from the casino than it advertises.

Quarter Chips: Worth $25, usually green in color.

Quarter Player: A player who wagers a minimum of $25 on each hand.

Rating: Method used by the pit to keep track of the amount of money wagered by a player for the purpose of establishing a comp value.

Red-Chip Player: A $5 bettor.

Reds: Chips in a casino valued at $5 (typically red).

Resplits: Allowing a player to resplit a pair, usually limited to three or four hands.

Rule of Six: In single-deck games, the number of rounds dealt before the shuffle equals six minus the number of players.

Risk of Ruin (ROR): The percentage chance of a player losing his bankroll. *See also* Lifetime Risk of Ruins.

S17: Dealer must stand on all 17s (including Soft 17). This rule is advantageous for the player.

Session Bankroll: Amount of bankroll required for a single sitting of play at a casino game.

Shoe: Device used to hold the undealt cards, usually when four or more decks of cards are used.

Sit 'n' Goes: Usually fast Internet tournaments.

Soft Hand: A hand containing an ace counted as 11.

Speed Count: A new and novel card-counting advantage-play method that tracks the ratio of 2s through 6s played per hand.

Splitting: A player choice available only when your first two cards are a pair or two 10-valued cards. A new card is dealt to each original card creating a new hand, and the player adds a new bet for the second hand. Each hand is now played separately (including more splits). Dissimilar face cards and 10s may be split as well, although it is not generally to the player's advantage to split 10-valued cards and is rarely done.

Stand: The player's decision not to receive any more cards (or the dealer requirement that he not draw any more cards).

Standard Deviation: A reflection of the variability of win or loss, or risk. A higher standard deviation means you will have more fluctuation in your bankroll as you play.

Stiff: A hard hand that totals 12 through 16. These are poor hands.

Surrender (a.k.a. Late Surrender): A playing option whereby a player can forfeit half of his bet and the right to complete his hand. You can surrender only after you receive your initial two cards and after the dealer checks if he has a blackjack.

Third Base: The playing seat located to the far left of the blackjack table, dealt last before the dealer (to the right of the dealer).

Trip Bankroll: An amount of bankroll required for a trip (consisting of more than one playing session).

Trip Risk of Ruin: The amount of money a player should bring for a single trip or session of blackjack, such as a weekend trip or evening of playing, to maintain less than a fixed chance risk of losing it (usually 5 percent). *See also* Lifetime Risk of Return and Risk of Ruin.

Toke: Another term for a tip.

Total Bankroll: The money a player uses for their entire lifetime of playing blackjack.

Unit Bet Size: The dollar value of your minimum bet.

Up-Card: The dealer's card (of the two initial cards) that is dealt face up for the players to see.

Variability: The ups and downs of your bankroll over time.

Win Rate: The average number of bet units won per round dealt. To convert this into an hourly win rate, multiply by your unit bet size and expected rounds per hour, generally 100.

About the Author

Frank Scoblete is the No. 1 best-selling gaming writer in America. He has written over 20 books and has also created audiotapes, videotapes, CDs, and DVDs.

Frank writes about all the casino games and has developed methods for getting real mathematical edges at craps, blackjack, Pai Gow poker, and even certain slot machines.

Frank has written for over 50 magazines, newspapers, and websites in America, Europe, Canada, and the Islands, including *Jackpot, Fun & Games, Midwest Gaming and Travel, Casino Player, Strictly Slots, CasinoCityTimes. com, Southern Gaming and Destinations, GoldenTouchCraps.com,* and *Gaming South.* He has also written several television shows.

He has appeared on many television shows on various networks, including the History Channel, the Travel Channel, TBS, the Discovery Channel, CNN, the Learning Channel, A&E, and the National Geographic Channel.

Frank has beaten the casinos for over 20 years and he has shared his knowledge and insights gained from such winning experience with millions of readers.